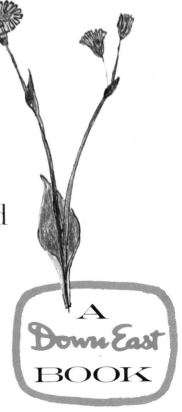

Spring
WILDFLOWERS
of New England

A
Down East
BOOK

$6.95

BLUE GIANT HYSSOP
see page 198

Spring
WILDFLOWERS
of
New England

By

Marilyn J. Dwelley

DOWN EAST ENTERPRISE, INC.

Camden, Maine

Spring
WILDFLOWERS
of New England

THIRD PRINTING

I dedicate this New England Wildflower book to my former students in China and Vassalboro, Maine, who have helped me to collect many of the specimens from which these drawings were made. It was their need for a simplified, but complete, study guide for spring wildflowers that prompted me to undertake this task. It was written so that beginners can learn to identify and enjoy our wildflowers. I have purposely omitted most of the scientific terms which botanists use to describe flowers. I hope that by using this book, children and amateurs alike will learn to identify our heritage of wildflowers, for in learning to know them, one also learns to love them as I have.

Marilyn J. Dwelley

PREFACE

The flowers in this book are arranged by color and are grouped into the following sections:

> White
> Pink or Red
> Orange
> Yellow
> Green
> Blue or Purple
> Brown

Because some flowers vary in color, they may be listed in two different sections. It may be necessary to look in more than one section to find a certain flower. For example a flower that is lavender might be in the pink or the purple section.

Within each color section, the flowers are arranged by families. The arrangement of families corresponds with that given in the 8th edition of GRAY'S MANUAL. Within the families the flowers are given according to GRAY'S order whenever possible. The order is disrupted some when several flowers are on one plate.

As my authority, I have used the NEW BRITTON AND BROWN ILLUSTRATED FLORA OF NORTH EASTERN UNITED STATES AND ADJACENT CANADA. When I have found a discrepancy in the Latin name for a certain flower, I have used the one given in BRITTON AND BROWN. In some instances, both of the Latin names were mentioned.

I would like to thank Dr. Charles D. Richards of the Botany Department at the University of Maine in Orono for all of his help and for the many hours he spent in checking my work for errors.

M. J. D.

CONTENTS

GLOSSARY

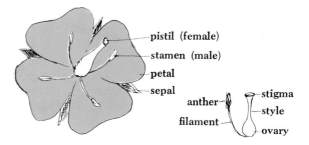

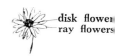

anther	The top or fertile part of the stamen.
axil	The angle formed where the leaf is attached to the stem.
basal	Located at the base of the plant.
blade	The large part of the petal or leaf.
bract	A small modified leaf — usually under the flower.
calyx	The whorl of sepals.
compound leaf	A leaf divided into smaller leaflets.
corolla	The whorl of petals.
entire	Without teeth or divisions.
mid vein	The central vein of a leaf running from base to tip.
pedicel	The stem or stalk for an individual flower.
perfoliate	The stem passes through the leaf.
petiole	The stalk on a leaf.
raceme	An unbranching flower cluster where each flower is on its own stem.
sheath	An organ or part of the leaf which surrounds the stem.
spike	A flower cluster where each flower is *not* on its own stem, but is attached directly to the main stem.
tendril	A twisting thread-like end used for climbing.
umbel	A flower cluster where all the flower stems start at the same point.
whorl	Three or more leaves in a circle around the stem.

WILD CALLA
Calla palustris
Arum Family

This is a slender plant which grows
from five to twelve inches in height.
It is often called Water Arum. It
used to be plentiful in bogs and
swamps of New England, but draining
practices and new highways have
almost eliminated this plant.
The upper surface of the spathe is
green and the inside of it is a waxy-
white. This beautiful spathe is often
mistaken for a flower, but the true
flowers are clustered together at the
end of the greenish yellow spadix
inside of the spathe. This cluster of
tiny flowers called the spadix is
usually from one to two inches long.
The beautiful dark green heart-
shaped leaves, which often reach a
width of four inches, stand above the
water in which the plant grows.
After the spathe dries up, a cluster
of red berries appears. This cluster of
red berries is quite similar to that
found on the Jack-in-the-pulpit.

STAR OF BETHLEHEM
Ornithogalum umbellatum
Lily Family

This plant has a tuft of narrow leaves
and a divided, leafless stalk which
grows from an underground bulb. The
grass-like leaves have a light-colored
or white midrib. The pictured
species grows in waste places, along
roadsides, near houses, and is often
cultivated. The stem is from four to
twelve inches tall. The flower is
waxy white on the inside, but is
striped with green on the outside.
The flower has six petals and is about
an inch across and only opens in
sunlight. The lower flower stalks are
often as long or longer than the top
middle one. This gives the appearance
of a rather flat-topped cluster.

COLICROOT or STARGRASS
Aletris farinosa
Lily Family

This plant has a cluster of narrow
basal leaves about eight inches
long around the leafless flower stalk.
Colicroot grows in dry sandy or
peaty soil to a height of from one
and one-half to three feet. At the
top of the stem is a raceme of small,
rough, white flowers, on short flower
stems (pedicles). The sepals and
petals are joined together to make a
tubular, six-toothed flower with a
swollen base. Each flower is nearly
one-half inch long.

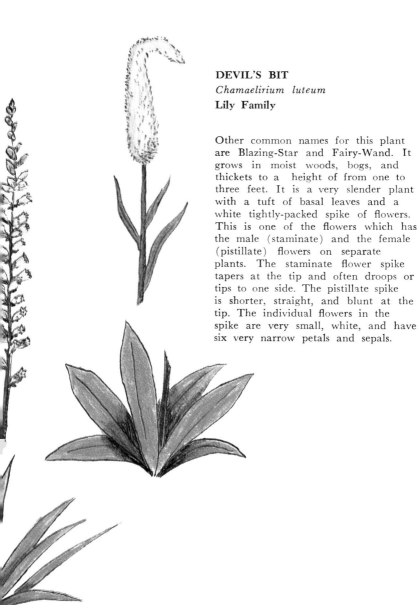

DEVIL'S BIT
Chamaelirium luteum
Lily Family

Other common names for this plant
are Blazing-Star and Fairy-Wand. It
grows in moist woods, bogs, and
thickets to a height of from one to
three feet. It is a very slender plant
with a tuft of basal leaves and a
white tightly-packed spike of flowers.
This is one of the flowers which has
the male (staminate) and the female
(pistillate) flowers on separate
plants. The staminate flower spike
tapers at the tip and often droops or
tips to one side. The pistillate spike
is shorter, straight, and blunt at the
tip. The individual flowers in the
spike are very small, white, and have
six very narrow petals and sepals.

THREE-LEAVED
FALSE SOLOMON'S SEAL
Smilacina trifolia
Lily Family

This plant is found in cold bogs or cool woods. It is from two to six inches high and has from two to four leaves — most frequently three. The leaf bases taper and sheathe the stem. The flowers have six points, and one produced in a few-flowered raceme at the end of the branch.

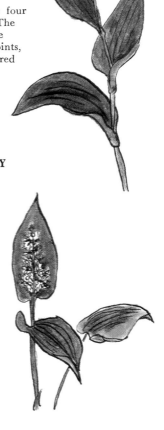

WILD LILY-OF-THE-VALLEY
Maianthemum canadense
Lily Family

This flower, also called Canada Mayflower, carpets large areas in forests or under trees along the roadsides. The plant usually has two leaves with heart-shaped bases, but sometimes has three. New plants coming up for the first time often have only one leaf and do not blossom. The stems are very slender and are often crooked at the point at which leaves are attached. The plant varies in height from two to eight inches. The white flowers are star-shaped, four lobed, and are arranged in a feathery cluster at the end of the stem. Pale red berries speckled with darker red follow the blossoms and provide wild birds with a good meal.

STARRY FALSE SOLOMON'S SEAL
Smilacina stellata
Lily Family

This plant is from eight to sixteen inches high and has eight to ten star-shaped flowers at the top. It grows on moist banks and is similar to the plant below. Leaves clasp the stem.

FALSE SOLOMON'S SEAL
Smilacina racemosa
Lily Family

This plant grows in moist woods and from one to three feet tall. It has crowded panicle of small white fragrant flowers. The stem is gracefully curving and has alternate oval pointed leaves. The leaves are three to six inches long and are coated with fine hair on the underside. The flowers have six petals and the stamens are quite prominent — giving a fuzzy appearance to the luster of flowers. The fruit is first whitish and speckled with brown, but later turns ruby-red.

13

PAINTED TRILLIUM
Trillium undulatum
Lily Family

This lovely member of the lily family
may be found in cool evergreen
woods and in mountain forests. It
opens its three wavy petals in May
or June. The three petals are
white with a v-shaped splash of
crimson or pink on them. This trillium
grows to be about a foot high, but
varies according to the richness of
the soil in which it grows.

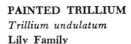

NODDING TRILLIUM
Trillium cernuum
Lily Family

This trillium grows in acid woods
to a height of fifteen to eighteen
inches. The flower dangles below the
three large umbrella-like leaves. The
flower is usually white, but may
be pink. The anthers which stick
out from the center are pink. The
leaves are deeply net veined and the
petals are recurved. The fruit is
a dark red berry.

LARGE FLOWERING TRILLIUM
Trillium grandiflorum
Lily Family

This White Trillium, like the other
trilliums in this book, is made up
of parts of three also. It has three
pointed green leaves, three sepals, three
waxy-white petals, a three-parted
pistil, and six (2 x 3) stamens.
The White Trillium may be found
blooming in May on the leafy floors
of rich, moist woodlands. It grows
to be more than fifteen inches high.
The radiant white flower is from
two to three inches across, but turns
a delicate pink as it begins to fade.
The flower gives off a
sweet-smelling odor, which is quite
different from the red or purple
trilliums which give off offensive
odors.

15

SMALL WHITE LADY'S SLIPPER
Cypripedium candidum
Orchid Family

This beautiful flower grows to a
height of six to twelve inches and is
found in boggy meadows or limestone
areas. It has three or four pointed
leaves (up to five inches long)
which ascend the stem. The side
petals and the sepals are greenish
brown spotted with purple. The
slipper lip or pouch is almost an inch
long and is waxy white with purple
stripes or veins inside.

SHOWY LADY'S SLIPPER
Cypripedium reginae
Orchid Family

This is perhaps our largest and most
showy wild flower. It has a stout
hairy stem which is leafy up to the
top. It is usually from one to three
feet high. The large leaves are
from three to eight inches long, and
the plant bears from one to three
flowers. The sepals are round or
oval and very waxy white in contrast
to the inflated lip which is variegated
with crimson and white stripes. The
lip is from one to two inches long.
This orchid grows in swamps and
open wet woods, and has been so
largely picked that it is close to
extinction in some areas. Do not pick
any members of the orchid family.

16

SMALL ROUND-LEAVED ORCHIS
Orchis rotundifolia
Orchid Family

This orchid is about eight or ten inches tall and grows in bogs, spruce forests, cold woods, and places where there is a peaty soil. It has only one broad oval basal leaf which is from one to three inches long. There are one or two scales sheathing the stem below the leaf. The flower is white with the larger bottom petal spreading and three lobed. The large white petal is spotted with purple or magenta. There are usually from five to ten flowers at the top of the stem, and each flower has its own small green bract beneath it.

WHITE ADDER'S MOUTH
Malaxis monophylla
Orchid Family

This orchid grows in damp woods and bogs to a height of from four to eight inches. There is a single, wide, pointed leaf at the base which clasps the stem. The flowers are greenish white and are arranged in a very slender tapering raceme. The horizontal petals are long and slender, but the lower lip is broadly heart-shaped and tapers to a long point. The top middle sepal stands erect behind the lip, but the bottom two sepals come out from behind the lower lip of the flower.

SPRING LADIES'-TRESSES
Spiranthes vernalis
Orchid Family

This Ladies'-Tresses blooms earlier than
most. It grows in wet meadows, bogs,
and marshes and along the coast.
It has a slender stem from six to
thirty-six inches tall and very
slender basal leaves which are
sometimes up to a foot long. The
flowers are entirely white or yellowish-
white, but have red hairs on them.
Each is about one-half inch long
and is very fragrant. The flowers are
close together in a dense raceme
which is often twisted into a spiral.
It is very downy
with fine,
simple
hairs.

WIDE-LEAVED
LADIES'-TRESSES
Spiranthes lucida
Orchid Family

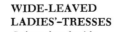

This orchid is from five to twelve
inches tall and grows in damp
woods, marshes, and along wet shores.
It has from three to five basal
leaves that are lance shaped. From
ten to fifteen flowers are crowded in
a dense spike with small scale-
like leaves beneath the flowers. The
flower is white, but the lower,
round, waxy lip has a broad spot
of yellow in the middle.

LIZARD'S TAIL or WATER DRAGON
Saururus cernuus
Lizard's-Tail Family

The Lizard's Tail grows in swamps, marshes, and in shallow water to a height of from two to five feet. The stem is very branching, but usually there are only a few flower spikes. Often, the branches without flower spikes are taller than the branches containing the spikes. Minute white flowers are fragrant and are arranged in a spike-like raceme which curves or droops down at the tip. The leaves are very large and heart-shaped. Each leaf has its own long leaf stem (petiole). The leaf stem forms a sheath around the main stem at the point where it joins the main stem.

BASTARD TOADFLAX
Comandra umbellata
Sandlewood Family

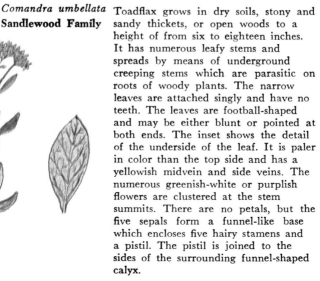

Toadflax grows in dry soils, stony and sandy thickets, or open woods to a height of from six to eighteen inches. It has numerous leafy stems and spreads by means of underground creeping stems which are parasitic on roots of woody plants. The narrow leaves are attached singly and have no teeth. The leaves are football-shaped and may be either blunt or pointed at both ends. The inset shows the detail of the underside of the leaf. It is paler in color than the top side and has a yellowish midvein and side veins. The numerous greenish-white or purplish flowers are clustered at the stem summits. There are no petals, but the five sepals form a funnel-like base which encloses five hairy stamens and a pistil. The pistil is joined to the sides of the surrounding funnel-shaped calyx.

19

COMMON CHICKWEED
Stellaria media
Pink Family

There are many kinds of chickweed but the one shown is most common. It grows as a weed in gardens, fields, and moist places to a height of from four to sixteen inches. The weak, reclining stems have pairs of small roundish leaves with pointed tips. The flowers (see enlargement) have five deeply notched white petals which are shorter than the sepals.

THYME-LEAVED SANDWORT
Arenaria serpyllifolia

This tiny plant grows in sandy soil and stony fields to a height of from two to eight inches. It has tiny, oval, pointed leaves about one-fourth of an inch long. The leaves are arranged in pairs on the wiry stem. The flower has five tiny rounded, unnotched, white petals which are shorter than the sepals.

MOUNTAIN SANDWORT
Arenaria groenlandica

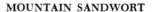

This looks similar to a chickweed, but the petals are only slightly notched. The very narrow basal leaves form tufts on the ground. It has five white petals which are longer than the sepals. Mountain Sandwort grows on or near rocks, especially in higher elevations, to a height of from two to five inches.

ᴸUNT-LEAVED SANDWORT or
ᴿOVE SANDWORT
ᵉnaria lateriflora

ᵒve Sandwort has five round white
notched petals and five smaller
ᵉen sepals. The oval leaves are
ᵒm one-half to one inch long and are
ᵉanged in uncrowded pairs along
ᵉ very slender stem. It grows in
ᵗ spots and in woodlands to a
ᵈght of from two to eight inches
ᵈ.

ᴱLD CHICKWEED
ᵉrastium arvense

ᵈis plant grows close to the ground
ᵈry, rocky places and reaches a
ᵈght of from four to sixteen
ᵗhes. The flowers are more than
ᵉ-half inch broad and have five
ᵈite petals with two lobes on
ᵗh petal.

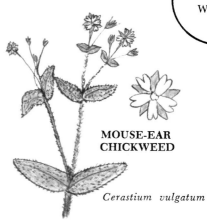

MOUSE-EAR
CHICKWEED

Cerastium vulgatum

This widely distributed chickweed
grows in waste places to a height of
from six to eighteen inches. It
has hairy stalkless leaves about three-
fourths of an inch long and the
stems are covered with sticky hairs.
The deeply notched petals are
about the same length as the sepals.

ROCK SANDWORT
Arenaria stricta

This sandwort has needle-like leaves
with tufts of shorter leaves in the
axils. The weak hairy branches are
often reclining on the ground
and form mats. The tiny white
flowers with five unnotched petals
have sepals which are much shorter. than
the petals. It grows in rocky soil
to a height of from four to
sixteen inches.

21

STARRY CAMPION
Silene stellata
Pink Family

Starry Campion is easily distinguished from other campions by the petals which are fringed at the outer edges. The leaves are in whorls of four instead of being paired. There is no inflated bladder.

EVENING LYCHNIS or WHITE CAMPION
Lychnis alba
Pink Family

This campion has fragrant white flowers which open at night, and their white forked petals are said to attract moths which spread the pollen from one flower to another. Five curved stamens protrude from the center. Lychnis grows in fields and waste places to a height of from one to three feet. It is a hairy, sticky plant.

This common flower grows in fields and along roadsides to a height of nearly three feet. It has many flowers in loose clusters at the ends the many branches. The unique part of this wild flower is the cup-shape calyx behind the white petals. It is tan or greenish and is inflated like a football. The veins are clearly visible on this calyx. Each flower has five petals, but each petal is so deeply notched that it looks like two Many stamens hang out from the center of the blossom. The leaves a from three to four inches long and are rounded at the base and pointed at the tip. They are arranged in pairs along the hairy stem of the plant.

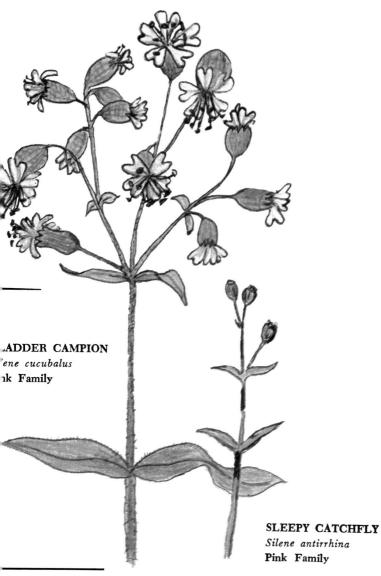

LADDER CAMPION
Silene cucubalus
Pink Family

SLEEPY CATCHFLY
Silene antirrhina
Pink Family

The petals may be either white or pink. See page 85 in the pink section for a description.

23

BUCKWHEAT
Fagopyrum esculentum
Smartweed Family

This plant is from eight to twenty-four
inches tall and is widespread in waste
places. The stem is smooth at the base,
but has lines of hairs at the top. The
leaves are broadly triangular in shape,
but have two lower lobes which point
in opposite directions. The lower leaves
are on long stems, but the upper
leaves have practically no petiole. The
flowers are white or pinkish and have a
five-parted calyx with sepals of
unequal width. The flowers are crowded
in compact clusters on long pedicels
which arise from axils of the leaves.
There is a swollen sheath where the leaf
is attached to the main stem. Sometimes
the stems are reddish.

FRAGRANT WATER-LILY
Nymphaea odorata
Water-lily Family

This gold-centered white flower m
be found floating on still ponds a
quiet waters. The leaf is large and
platter-like with a deep slit on one
side. It is shiny green on top, but
is often purple on the underside.
flowers are from three to five inche
across and are very fragrant. The
petals are pointed and tapering,
but diminish in size towards the
center of the plant.

TUBEROUS WATER-LILY
Nymphaea tuberosa
Water-lily Family

The Tuberous Water-Lily is similar to
the lily above, but it is not fragrant.
The leaves are green on the
underside. The white petals are more
rounded instead of being pointed.

White
Baneberry
Berries
Actaea pachypoda

RED BANEBERRY
Actaea rubra
Buttercup Family

The Red Baneberry grows to be between one and two feet in height. It can be found growing in shaded woodlands and thickets. If there is a woodland spring or stream nearby, one is likely to find a Red Baneberry growing in the shadows beside it.

The tiny white flowers are arranged in a dense cluster at the end of the stem. Each individual flower has from four to ten petals and numerous white stamens which tend to give it a feathery appearance when viewed from a distance.

After the flowers have gone by, a cluster of scarlet-red poisonous berries appears. Each berry has a black dot at the end, is on its own separate stem, and is about one-half inch long.

The leaves are pointed and sharply toothed with either rounded or pointed teeth. The leaves are arranged in groups of three and the veins on the leaves are very noticeable.

A similar flower, the *White Baneberry,* has leaves and flowers very similar to the one above. The big difference is the berries. These are pure white with a black dot at the end of each one. They are born on thick, bright red stalks. The cluster of flowers on the Red Baneberry is quite round, while the cluster of flowers on the White Baneberry is more like a cylinder.

25

FALSE
RUE-ANEMONE
Isopyrum biternatum
Buttercup Family

RUE ANEMONE
Anemonella thalictroides
Buttercup Family

This delicate early spring flower can be distinguished from the wood anemone because it has a cluster of blossoms above the whorl of leaves — not just one. It has wiry, black stalks bearing leaves in groups of three leaflets with each leaflet again being divided into three parts. From among the whorl of leaves, several slender black flowering stalks arise and each bears one white to pinkish flower with from six to ten showy white sepals. Numerous stamens form a yellow, lacy center.

This delicate plant grows in moist woods and thickets to a height of about six inches. The flower is white and has five petal-like sepals and numerous flat, white-stalked stamens in the center.

The three-parted leaves are compound. From one to few flowers are at the ends of the stem. These flowers are usually one-half to three-fourths of an inch across.

GOLDTHREAD
Coptis groenlandica
Buttercup Family

Goldthread is a small plant from three to six inches tall which grows from a thin yellow underground stem which looks like a root. This "root" has been used for dyes and medicines and is said to be helpful in curing canker sores if chewed. Several leafless stalks grow on each plant and each bears a single flower at the tip. The flower is about three-fourths of an inch broad and has from five to seven showy white sepals and insignificant small, club-like petals. The showy sepals are white inside, but are often shaded with brown or gray on the back. The shiny evergreen leaves have three wedge-shaped parts and the underside is a paler color.

White

THIMBLEWEED
Anemone virginiana
Buttercup Family

There are several thimbleweeds in our area and they can be distinguished only by technical, botanical inspection. The one shown grows in open woods, thickets, and clearings and is less than three feet tall. It has hairy dark green leaves that are heavily veined. On the lower, larger leaves (not shown) the segments of the leaf blades curb towards the base. The flower is at the top of the stout stem and is from two-thirds to one and one-half inches broad. It has five greenish-white sepals that look like petals. The receptacle on which the flower rests grows larger after the flower fades and becomes thimble-shaped.

WOOD ANEMONE or WINDFLOWER

Anemone quinquefolia
Buttercup Family

This low delicate woodland plant bears a single flower above the circle of drooping leaves on the stem. Each leaf is divided into from three to five segments. The flower has from four to nine (usually five) white sepals which look like petals. The outside is often tinged with pale pink. Usually the flower is in a partially closed position, but on sunny days opens widely to display a cluster of fragile yellow stamens in the center.

27

BLACK COHOSH or BUGBANE
Cimcifuga racemosa
Buttercup Family

Bugbane grows in moist shady woods
to a height of from three to eight
feet. It has enormous, stalked leaves
which are divided into sets of three,
then are re-divided into sets of three
toothed, cut, leaflets. One leaf is so
large and has so many divided leaflets,
that one might think it is a large branch
with many leaves. A wand-like spike
of white flowers towers high above the
leaves. These flowers have a very
unpleasant odor — even to insects which
appear to avoid the plant. The four
or five white petal-like sepals fall early
and leave bushy tufts of numerous
stamens centered by a single pistil.
This pistil becomes a small seed pod
which makes an odd rattling sound
when it is dried.

WHITE WATER-BUTTERCUP or WHITE WATER-CROWFOOT
Ranunculus longirostris
Buttercup Family

This water plant has a small five-petaled
flower which looks like a white
buttercup, and indeed, the two are
related. The flower rests on the surface
of the water of ponds or slow-moving
streams. The rest of the plant is
submerged. The stem is often as long
as a foot or more, and the tufts of
feathery leaves, are attached directly to
the stem.

MAY-APPLE or MANDRAKE
Podophyllum peltatum
Barberry Family

The May-Apple has a crotched stem and very large umbrella-like leaves which are often as wide as one foot. It grows to a height of one to one and one-half feet, and where it is abundant, covers large areas of forest floors. From the crotch in the stem grows a single, large, waxy-white flower about two inches broad. The sweet-smelling flower has from six to nine large petals, twice as many stamens, and a large central pistil. The ovary at the bottom of this pistil develops into a lemon-like berry which is edible if prepared properly. The seeds and other parts of this plant are poisonous.

TWINLEAF
Jeffersonia diphylla
Barberry Family

The large white blossom of the Twinleaf is very similar to that of the Bloodroot, but this plant is easily identified by its leaves. Each leaf is parted into two equal, lobed divisions. This woodland plant is from five to eight inches tall while in bloom, but later grows as high as eighteen inches. The single white flower grows on a leafless stem. There are eight petals, eight stamens, and four sepals which drop soon after the flower opens. The white flower is about an inch broad.

DUTCHMAN'S BREECHES
Dicentra cucullaria
Poppy Family

Early in April in rich woodlands, one may find patches of pale sage-green leaves which have three parts and are very deeply and raggedly cut. These feathery leaves will undoubtedly belong to a peculiar wild flower called the Dutchman's Breeches.

When the leaves are completely filled out, the root sends forth a thin flower stalk from five to nine inches tall. From this stalk little cream-colored flowers with yellow tips will form. There will be from four to eight inverted flowers which look like tiny pairs of breeches or pantaloons hanging upside down on a line. The four large white petals have inflated spurs at the top which are paired to form legs while the two lower parts seem to protect the stigma of the pistil which protrudes below.

SQUIRREL-CORN
Dicentra canadensis
Poppy Family

Similar to the Dutchman's Breeches is Squirrel-Corn. This flower is also found in rich woodlands or at the edges of the woods. The spurs on the Squirrel-Corn are short and rounded at the top — not elongated as in Dutchman's Breeches. The flowers are a greenish white and sometimes have a touch of pink at the edges.

The leaves are very similar to the Dutchman's Breeches, but the root stalk is very different. This plant has roots with tubers or swellings on them which resemble whole-kernel corn.

BLOODROOT
Sanguinaria canadensis
Poppy Family

Bloodroot grows on dry rocky slopes or along streams in open rich woodlands. Usually there is a large patch rather than one single plant. The single, showy flower is at the top of a leafless orange stem which is from six to twelve inches tall. The flower is as large as one and one-half inches broad. The flower has two sepals when in bud, but looses them before it is in full bloom. The single, deeply lobed, veined leaf is wrapped around the buds for protection and opens wide after the flower is in full bloom. When the flower fades, the leaf grows larger — often as large as eight inches in width. The stem and root produce a red-orange juice when broken. The number of white petals varies from eight to twelve, but usually there will be a wide petal and a narrower petal alternating around the orange center.

SICKLE-POD
Arabis canadensis
Mustard Family

Sickle-pod is a stout, erect plant which grows in moist or dry woods to a height of from one to three feet. It has small white flowers with four petals. The leaves are long, narrow and downy and have toothed edges. A distinctive characteristic is the curved seed pods which hang down.

HAIRY ROCK CRESS
Arabis hirsuta
Mustard Family

This erect hairy plant grows on ledges or rocky cliffs to a height of from four to twelve inches. It has oblong-shaped or paddle-shaped leaves in a circle at the base of the stem and narrow leaves which clasp the stem. The flowers are white and have four petals. Long, flat seed pods form after flowers fade.

SMOOTH ROCK CRESS
Arabis laevigata
Mustard Family

Smooth Rock Cress is a smooth gray-green plant with no hairs — except perhaps on the basal leaves which might be scarcely hairy. It grows in moist or dry woods, on rocky ledges, and on hillsides to a height of from one to three feet. The white flowers are about the same as most other members of the mustard family, but the distinctive characteristic to help in identification is the leaves which have lobed bases and grasp the stem. The seed pods are usually horizontal, but may curve downward. They are rarely straight.

LYRE-LEAVED ROCK CRESS
Arabis lyrata
Mustard Family

This Rock Cress grows in dry woods, fields, and sandy soil to a height of from four to sixteen inches. It is very similar to the others of this group, but has two distinctive characteristics. The basal leaves are deeply lobed and the upper leaves are narrow and do not clasp the stem.

33

WHITLOW GRASS
Draba verna
Mustard Family

Whitlow Grass is a small plant with a
circle of long hairy leaves at the
base. It grows in waste places and
along roads to a height of from
one to five inches. There are several
very slender leafless stalks which
bear flowers at the top. The tiny
flowers are white and have four deeply
cut petals. Typically, and as
in the case of the other mustards on
preceeding pages, the buds at the
bottom open first, a few at a time.
As the flowers fade, oval seed pods
develop. The top of the stem elongates
as more and more of the buds open.

HOARY ALYSSUM
Berteroa incana
Mustard Family

Hoary Alyssum is a hairy plant with
stiff branched stems. It grows as a
weed in waste places to a height
of from one to two feet. The leaves
are alternate on the stem and are
long and untoothed. The tiny white
flowers have four deeply notched
petals. Eliptical hairy seedpods with a
point at the tip develop as the
flowers fade.

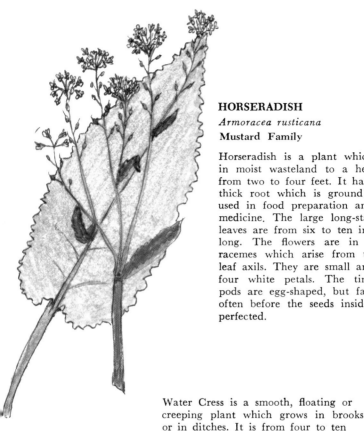

HORSERADISH
Armoracea rusticana
Mustard Family

Horseradish is a plant which grows in moist wasteland to a height of from two to four feet. It has a thick root which is ground up and used in food preparation and as a medicine. The large long-stalked basal leaves are from six to ten inches long. The flowers are in terminal racemes which arise from the upper leaf axils. They are small and have four white petals. The tiny seed pods are egg-shaped, but fall early, often before the seeds inside are perfected.

TRUE WATER CRESS
Nasturtium officinale
Mustard Family

Water Cress is a smooth, floating or creeping plant which grows in brooks or in ditches. It is from four to ten inches high. The tiny white flowers have four petals and are from one-half to one and one-third inches long. The juicy oval leaves are divided into from three to nine parts, but most leaves have five parts. These oval leaves have a pungent refreshing taste and are used in salads, sandwiches, or as a garnish for foods.

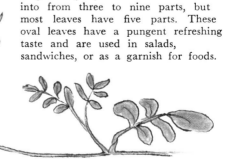

35

FIELD PENNY-CRESS
Thlaspi arvense
Mustard Family

Field Penny-cress is a common weed. It has wide–toothed leaves on the stem and no basal leaves. The four-petaled white flowers line the top of the stem and open from the bottom upwards. As the flowers fade, a flat, round, deeply notched seed pod appears. The pod is nearly one-half inch broad when mature and is winged. Several seeds are in each of the two cells.

SPRING CRESS
Cardamine bulbosa
Mustard Family

Spring Cress grows in wet places. It is from six to twenty-four inches high and has four-petaled white flowers about one-half inch long. The identifying feature of this plant is the roundish basal leaves with long leaf stalks. These contrast greatly with the leaves along the stem which are toothed and have *no* stalks at all. The seed pods which develop after the flowers fade are long, slender, and pointed at the tip.

The Shepherd's Purse is an insignificant weed of waste places. It grows to a height of from six to twenty inches. There is a circle of dandelion-like leaves at the bottom and toothed leaves on the stem. The flower stalk contains many flowers on short stems which branch off from the main stalk. The bottom buds open first. Each tiny flower (1/12 inch broad) is white and has four petals. As the flowers fade, a triangular seed pod forms. The seed has a center seam and the two halves are puffed out like a purse.

SHEPHERD'S PURSE
Capsella bursa-pastoris
Mustard Family

SLENDER-LEAVED SUNDEW
Drosera linearis
Sundew Family

The leaves of this Sundew are very narrow and are usually longer than the flower-bearing stalk. There are from one to four white flowers on each plant, often solitary on individual flower stalks. It grows in bogs and wet sand to a height of from two to five inches.

ROUND-LEAVED SUNDEW
Drosera rotundifolia
Sundew Family

his plant grows in acid or peaty soil bogs and swamps to a height of om four to twelve inches. Usually ndew plants grow close together in it-like clusters. The small, round ives are at the base of the plant long slender stalks. Each leaf is vered with reddish glandular irs which give off moisture like tiny w drops. The leafless flower stalk ars from three to fifteen flowers iich have five white petals and a eenish "eye."

SPATULATE-LEAVED SUNDEW
Drosera intermedia
Sundew Family

This Sundew has longer, more oval shaped leaves. The blades are up to an inch long and are broader towards the tip. The leaf stems are smooth and erect and up to two inches long. This Sundew grows in acid bogs — especially near the coast — to a height of from two to eight inches. The leaves are in a circle at the base of the flower stem and have glandular hairs only on the upper surface. The flowers are white and are born on leafless flower stalks.

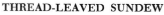

THREAD-LEAVED SUNDEW
Drosera filiformis
Sundew Family

is sundew has sticky glandular irs on erect string-like leaves. The all purplish-white flowers are on a g, curved stalk. They begin to open the bottom and open a few at time. The plant is from eight to ten hes tall and grows in damp sand coastal plains.

37

MITREWORT
Mitella diphylla
Saxifrage Family

In late April and on into May and June, this delicate lacy flower can be found in woodlands from Nova Scotia to Minnesota and southward. The slender flower stalk is very hairy and grows to a height of eleven or twelve inches. At the end of this flower stalk, there is a raceme of fine white flowers, each on its own little stem. The orange stamens can be easily seen protruding from each of the little flowers, giving it a feathery appearance from a distance.

The leaves are close to the ground and are similar in appearance to a maple leaf. These dark green leaves have fine hairs on their upper sides and sometimes are mottled with brown. Because of this plant's similarity to the Mitrewort and the two leaved Mitrewort, it is often called the *False Mitrewort*.

FOAM FLOWER
Tiarella cordifolia
Saxifrage Family

Another common name for this plant is Bishop's Cap, and upon close inspection of the flower capsule, one can see the likeness. The Mitrewort grows in rich damp woods to a height of from eight to eighteen inches. Halfway up the hairy flower stalk are two leaves opposite each other. They have no leaf stalk, but the dark green basal leaves have long leaf stalks. The raceme of small, white, dainty flowers has a feathery look because of the fringe petals. The leaves are deeply toothed and shaped like those from a maple tree.

EARLY SAXIFRAGE
Saxifraga virginiensis
Saxifrage Family

Early Saxifrage grows in dry, rocky fields and woods. It flowers early when it is only about four inches tall, but later grows to a height of about sixteen inches. The stem is light in color and is often sticky and hairy. Hairy, basal leaves surround the stem. These are nearly as broad as they are long. The flowers are in clusters which branch off from the main stem. Each small flower has five white petals and ten bright yellow stamens protruding from the center.

SWAMP SAXIFRAGE
Saxifraga pensylvanica
Saxifrage Family

Swamp Saxifrage is a plant with erect, leafless stems from twelve to forty inches high. It grows in wet meadows, bogs, and swamps. The basal leaves are long and narrow — often as long as eight inches. The tiny flowers have five greenish-white petals and ten stamens and are arranged in tight clusters which are arranged alternately along the stem. Each cluster has its own shorter stem branching from the main stem.

THREE-TOOTHED CINQUEFOIL
Potentilla tridentata
Rose Family

The Three-Toothed Cinquefoil is a tiny plant which grows in great patches at high elevations and on dry, rocky slopes. It has white blossoms with many long yellow stamens. The leaves are mostly near the base. Each is divided into three segments which are three-toothed at the end. These leaves turn deep red in the fall.

DEWDROP
Dalibarda repens
Rose Family

False Violet or Dalibarda are other names given to this low, spreading plant. It grows in rich woods to a height of from two to five inches. The downy leaves are nearly round and have finely scalloped edges. They are on long petioles (leaf stems). The flowers are on separate reddish stalks. Each flower is about one-half inch broad, has five petals, and a tuft of bushy stamens in the center.

BAKED-APPLE BERRY or CLOUDBERRY
Rubus chamaemorus
Rose Family

This plant grows in bogs and on wet mountain slopes. It has creeping underground stems from which erect stalks grow to a height of from three to eight inches. The solitary flower has white petals and a tuft of numerous yellow-tipped stamens in the center. It commonly has two or three broad five-lobed leaves with toothed margins. The fruit is a peach-colored, red-orange, or yellow berry which is edible, and has the flavor of baked apples.

WILD STRAWBERRY
Fragaria virginiana
Rose Family

This plant, with its five-petaled white blossoms and deeply-toothed three-parted leaves is a familiar sight to all who have ever been in New England in the spring. They grow in profusion in open fields, along paths, and in sunny spots at the edges of woods. Each white blossom has five round white petals, a bright yellow center, and five lighter green sepals which can be seen between each petal. As the flower fades, the center gets larger, turns green, and then ripens to a scarlet, delicious strawberry. The taste of the berries differs with the amount of rain and sunshine, but the flavor far surpasses cultivated strawberries. The hairy, coarsely-toothed leaves are in sets of three, and the stems are hairy. This strawberry can be identified by the small seeds embedded in pits in the fruit.

WHITE AVENS
Geum canadense
Rose Family

White Avens is a straggling, branching plant which is up to four feet tall. It can be either smooth or hairy. The principal leaves have three pointed segments, but the upper ones may be simple and the lower ones may have five parts. The flowers are replaced by bristly seed-like fruits, each section of which has a tiny "tail" which is formed by the styles. This plant grows at edges of woods and in thickets.

41

There are over two hundred species of blackberries in our area. Most of the plants have woody, prickly stems and leaves which are divided into pointed segments with toothed margins. The one shown here is a creeping variety which grows in dry places and sandy soil.

BLACKBERRY or BRAMBLE
Rose Family

LOW-RUNNING BLACKBERRY or NORTHERN DEWBERRY
Rubus flagellaris
Rose Family

This blackberry has horizontal stems which trail on or near the surface of the ground to a length of several feet. The stems are not bristly, but on some plants the stems have curved spines. The branches grow upright from the creeping stems to a height of from four to twelve inches and are often prickly or hairy. The leaves are divided into from three to seven thin leaflets, but the most common is three. The sharply toothed leaflets have points at the tips but are rounded at the base. The white flowers are nearly one inch across and have five petals which are slightly longer than the five green sepals. Numerous stamens in the center of the flower give it a tufted, fuzzy appearance. The fruit is a black berry which is very tasty, but has large seeds. The berry varies in size from one-half to one inch long.

RED RASPBERRY
Rubus strigosus
Rose Family

The Red Raspberry has erect or reclining stems up to two and one-half feet tall and grows in dry or moist woods, fields and along old logging areas where remains of lumbering operations cause new growth to be lush and green. The stems have slender spines and stiff bristles on them. The leaves are divided into three or five toothed leaflets with gray hairs on the underside. The white flowers have five petals, five green sepals, and numerous stamens. The fruit is red and very delicious to eat.

DIAPENSIA
Diapensia lapponica
Diapensia Family

Diapensia forms low, leafy, evergreen mats on rocks of high elevations. The mat is usually less than four inches tall. The stems are woody and are crowded with opposite, flat, blunt, unlobed leaves less than one-half inch long. The pretty white flowers rise above the leafy mats on short stalks. The corolla is a white, erect bell with a margin of five roundish lobes. The five yellow-tipped stamens are fastened between the five lobes of the flower.

SHADBUSH
Amelanchier canadensis
Rose Family

This bushy shrub or small tree grows in swamps and wet woods to a height of few to twenty-five feet. Other names for it are Shad-blow, Service Berry, June Berry, Sugar Plum, and Swamp Cherry. The alternate leaves are egg-shaped with pointed tips and tiny teeth at the margins, but these are not fully developed at flowering time. The white flowers have five long, narrow petals and numerous center stamens. They are in large clusters and seem to bloom at about the same time — thus giving a dazzling, fuzzy-white appearance of white mist to the otherwise lifeless woods around them. The fruit is nearly one-half inch in diameter, red at first, but turns to dark purple when fully ripe. It looks like a miniature apple and is sweet and juicy. Because of the large seeds and rough-textured blossom end, they are not good for pies. They have excellent eating quality when eaten raw.

CHOKEBERRY
Aronia melanocarpa
Rose Family

This low shrub grows in acid soil of bogs, dunes, woods and rocks to a height of a few inches to two feet. The flowers have five round petals and numerous stamens. The finely toothed leaves alternate along the stem but vary in size, from one-half to two inches long. The leaves are dark green above and pale underneath. The black fruit is about one-third inch in diameter and hang in small clusters. The berries are juicy, but are tart until they are cooked.

This shrub grows in woods, swamps, and along paths and roads — sometimes reaching a height of thirty feet. The flowers are very tiny, and are arranged in thick, cylinder-shaped clusters from three to six inches long. The thin leaves are from two to five inches long, are alternate, and have sharply toothed margins. The fruit is dark red in long, loose clusters. They are inedible as berries, but make excellent jelly.

CHOKECHERRY
Prunus virginiana
Rose Family

44

This widely branched shrub or small tree grows in moist or dry woods to a height of from ten to thirty feet. What appear to be four notched white petals are really bracts. The true flowers are in the center of these bracts in a cluster of from twenty to thirty flowers. The leaves are broad, about half as wide as long, but narrow to a point at the tip. The underside of the leaf is a paler color. The leaves and berries both turn scarlet in the fall.

DOGWOOD
Cornus florida
Dogwood Family

ALSIKE CLOVER
Trifolium hybridum
Pea Family

This clover has smooth stems from one to three feet tall. It grows along roads and in fields. The leaf segments are in sets of three, are elliptical in shape, and do not have the light-colored triangle on them that the white clover does. The flowers are creamy white tinged with peach color, but very quickly fade and turn brown.

This clover grows along roadsides and in waste lands to a height of from two to eight feet. The leaves are divided into three narrow clover-like leaflets which are rarely longer than one inch. These are toothed on the outer half and are very fragrant when crushed. The small white flowers are arranged in numerous slender, tapering clusters which grow from leaf axils. Each individual flower is not more than one-fourth of an inch in length.

WHITE SWEET-CLOVER
Melilotus alba
Pea Family

This is the common clover found on lawns and in fields. The flowers and leaves are on separate stalks arising from creeping runners. The leaf-segments are broad, toothed, and usually have a pale triangular-shaped mark on each leaflet. The flowers are tiny and pea-like, but are arranged in roundish heads. They turn from white to pinkish to brown as they age and turn downward.

WHITE CLOVER
Trifolium repens
Pea Family

45

SENECA SNAKEROOT
Polygala senega
Milkwort Family

Seneca Snakeroot grows in dry or moist woods and rocky places to a height of from six to eighteen inches. There are usually several upright stems originating from the same base. The tiny white flowers are pea-like with broad white wings. They are arranged in a slender, dense terminal cluster. Narrow lance-shaped leaves are attached singly to the stem.

WHITE VERVAIN
Verbena urticifolia
Vervain Family

White Vervain is a straggling, unattractive weedy species which grows at edges of woods, in fields, and in waste places to a height of from three to five feet. It sometimes has only a simple stem, but most often it is branching at the base. It has coarsely toothed leaves on short stalks and the blades of the leaves are often blotched with mildew. Tiny white flowers one-twelfth of an inch across are sparsely arranged on upright, thread-like spikes.

CANADA VIOLET
Viola canadensis
Violet Family

This violet grows in deep woods or woodlands to a height of from eight to sixteen inches. It has leafy stems and many flowers. It grows profusely and is easily transplanted to flower gardens. The heart-shaped leaves have toothed margins and the flowers are fragrant. The inside of the petals is white, but the outside is tinged with lavender or pale purple. The center of the flower is yellow, and the lower petals are purple-veined. Only the two side petals are bearded. The stems are usually forked, hairy, and are sometimes purplish in color.

46

This hairless violet may be identified by its long, narrow leaves with the tapering base. The reddish flower-bearing stalks are taller than the leaves. It grows in wet meadows, bogs and on shores to a height of from two to six inches. The five white petals all lack beards and the three lowest petals are striped with brown-purple veins.

LANCE-LEAVED VIOLET
Viola lancelata
Violet Family

This violet has smooth flower and leaf stalks which rise from slender, underground, creeping stems. The leafblades are a dark green with a satiny sheen. They have a heart-shaped base but are pointed at the tip. The underside of the leaves is smooth, but there are usually minute hairs on the upper surface — especially on the base. The white flowers are very fragrant. The three lower petals have brown-purple veins near the base, and all five petals are beardless.

SWEET WHITE VIOLET
Viola lanceolata
Violet Family

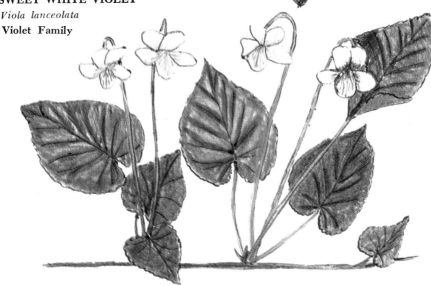

WILD SARSAPARILLA
Aralia nudicaulis
Ginseng Family

This plant has one large umbrella-
like leaf which is divided into three
segments and then divided again
to give the appearance of a leafy
branch. The single leafless flowering
stem is shorter than the leaf stem
and is also divided — usually into
threes but up to seven parts. Each part
bears a round, ball-like cluster
(umbel) at the tip. The individual
flowers in this umbel are greenish
white with five turned-back petals in
a cup-shaped calyx. Five white stamens
protrude from each flower and give
the umbels a fuzzy appearance.
Wild Sarsaparilla grows in open
woods to a height of from eight to
sixteen inches.

BRISTLY SARSAPARILLA

Aralia hispida
Ginseng Family

This Sarsaparilla is easily distinguished
from the one above by the bristles on
the woody stem. The plant is larger
and more branching. The stem bears
several leaves which are divided
into segments. The umbels *are not* on
separate stalks, but attached right
to the leaf-bearing stems. This plant
grows in dry woods and along
roadsides and railroad beds to a
height of from one to three feet.

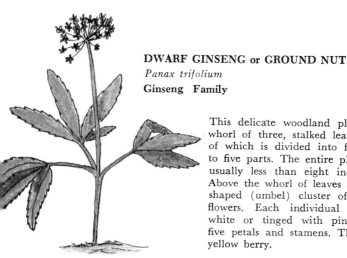

DWARF GINSENG or GROUND NUT
Panax trifolium
Ginseng Family

This delicate woodland plant has a whorl of three, stalked leaves, each of which is divided into from three to five parts. The entire plant is usually less than eight inches high. Above the whorl of leaves is a ball-shaped (umbel) cluster of white flowers. Each individual flower is white or tinged with pink and has five petals and stamens. The fruit is a yellow berry.

Purple Angelica is a very large plant — sometimes as tall as nine feet. It grows along streams and in swamps or wet woods. It has a dark purple stem and the stalks of the upper leaves have a papery swollen sheath which almost encircles the stem. The leaf branch is *attached to this sheath,* not to the main stem itself. This branch has three smaller branches, and then each is re-divided into five sharply-toothed, uneven leaflets of differing shapes and sizes. The tiny white flowers are in umbels from four to eight inches across. The umbels are also re-divided into from twenty to forty-five smaller umbels. This is called a compound umbel.

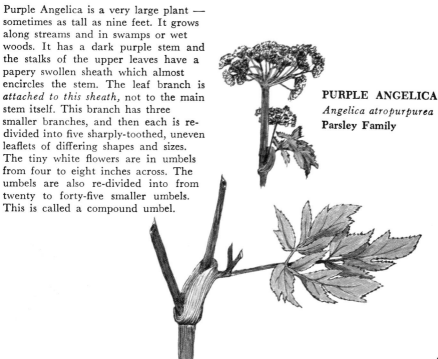

PURPLE ANGELICA
Angelica atropurpurea
Parsley Family

CARAWAY
Carum carvi
Parsley Family

This plant grows in waste places to a height of from one to two feet. It has umbels of small white flowers both at the tops of the plant and in between leaf stalks. The stems are hollow and hairless and the leaves are very narrowly cut. There are two distinctive characteristics which make it differ from the other flowers on this page. The slightly curved, ribbed seeds, which are aromatic and used in cooking, is one. The other is the fact that the flower cluster does not have leaf bracts under it as do the others.

FOOL'S PARSLEY
Aethusa cynapium
Parsley Family

This plant is smaller, usually less than two feet tall. It grows in fields and waste places. It is poisonous and ill-smelling and has shiny leaves. A distinctive characteristic is the set of long bracts that hang downward like a beard below each secondary flower cluster.

POISON HEMLOCK
Conium maculatum
Parsley Family

This is a large branching plant found in wastelands growing to a height of from two to six feet. It has dark green fern-like leaves which are broadly triangular in general outline but are deeply cut. The stems are hollow, grooved and are spotted with purple, and have a very unpleasant odor when crushed. The juice is poisonous.

**QUEEN
ANNE'S
LACE**
Daucus carota
Parsley Family

This plant has many names. **Wild
Carrot, Bird's Nest,** and **Queen Anne's
Lace** are only a few. It grows in
fields and dry waste places to a height
of from one to four feet. It has flat-
topped clusters of tiny white five-
petaled flowers. Usually there are one or
two tiny sterile purple flowers in
the center of the flat head.
This plant is hated by dairy farmers,
because it gives an unpleasant flavor to
milk produced by cows who eat it.
Note the three stiff green bracts below
the flower head. These curve upwards
and the outer edges of the cluster
curl to form a cup-shaped bunch of
brown wool resembling a bird's nest
when the flower goes to seed.

SCOTCH LOVAGE
Ligusticum scothicum
Parsley Family

This plant has stout purple stems which
are more or less branched. It grows
along rocky and sandy seashores to
a height of twelve to twenty-four
inches. The shiny, thick leaves are
nine-parted and are grouped in sets
of three pointed, sharply-toothed
leaflets. The white flowers are tiny
and are grouped in umbels at the
top of the plant and at the end of the
branches. Each umbel is in turn
divided into smaller umbels.

51

SWEET CICELY
Osmorhiza claytoni
Parsley Family

This soft, hairy plant has a round
stem and wide leaves with three main
parts. Each part is re-divided into
toothed segments. Sweet Cicely grows
in rich woods and along wet
roadsides to a height of from one and
a half to three feet. The lower leaves
are often more than a foot long.
The stem and roots emit a licorice-like
or anise-like odor when crushed. The
minute white flowers are arranged in
small umbels with only a small
number of flowers in each umbel. The
fruits are long, narrow, and ribbed.
When viewed through a magnifying
glass, the sharp hairs lying flat along
the ribs may be seen.

HARBINGER OF SPRING or PEPPER AND SALT
Erigenia bulbosa
Parsley Family

This smooth, delicate plant grows in
rich woods from a bulb-like tuber
to a .height of from four to nine
inches. The leaves are usually
undeveloped at flowering time and the
umbel of flowers tops the stem about
six inches above the ground. When
the flat seeds develop, two leaves
unfold. They are finely cut into three
main parts and each part is re-divided
into narrow segments. The flowers
have five flat white petals and red-
brown or black stamens and are
arranged in umbels with leafy bracts
at the base.

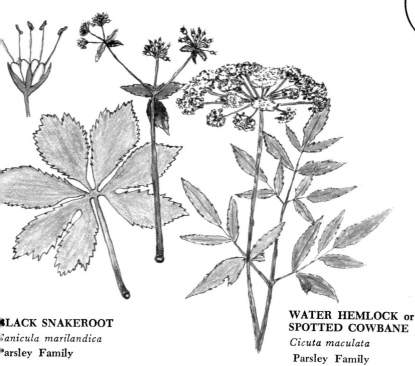

BLACK SNAKEROOT
Sanicula marilandica
Parsley Family

This plant grows in thickets and rich woods to a height of from one to four feet. It has a hollow stem and long-stalked blue-green leaves. They are divided into five parts, but the two lower leaflets are so deeply lobed that it has the appearance of seven parts. The tiny flowers are greenish-white and are arranged in small uneven umbels. There are leafy bracts at the base of these umbels. The fruit is an oval-shaped bur with many hooked bristles on it.

The green sepals are nearly the same length as the white petals, but the stamens protrude far out.

WATER HEMLOCK or SPOTTED COWBANE
Cicuta maculata
Parsley Family

This poisonous plant grows in wet meadows, ditches, and swamps to a height of from three to six feet. It has a smooth, stout, much-branched stem that is streaked with purple. The leaves are divided into two or three sections and each section is re-divided into many coarsely toothed, pointed leaflets which are often tinged with red. The illustration shows one entire leaf with its many leaflets. A distinctive characteristic to help in identifying this plant is the veins in the leaflets. They run from the midrib to the notches *between* the teeth — not to the tips of the teeth as on most leaves. The flowers are tiny and have five tiny petals. They are arranged in numerous umbels above the leafy portion of the plant. The umbels are sometimes as large as four inches across.

53

BUNCHBERRY
Cornus canadensis
Dogwood Family

The Bunchberry is a beautiful little herb which grows in large patches in cool woodlands all across the northern United States and Canada. It may be found blooming from May to July. A first glance would tell us that the flower has four white petals, but this is not true. The Bunchberry has tiny greenish flowers in the center of four large white bracts, which appear to be the petals of a flower.

From six to eight large, pointed green leaves are arranged in a circle around the stem. From the center of this green circle of leaves grows a tiny stem which supports the four white bracts and a tiny insignificant cluster of greenish-white blossoms in the center. These are the true flowers.

The whole plant seldom reaches a height of more than six or eight inches.

When the flowers fade, a cluster of brilliant red berries forms above th whorl of leaves. This gives a very attractive appearance to the tiny plant. The berries are edible, though many consider them tasteless. They are qui seedy, and not good for pies.

TRAILING ARBUTUS
Epigaea repens
Heath Family

See page 106
in the pink section
for full description.

54

GIANT BIRD'S-NEST or PINEDROPS
Pterosporo andromedea
Heath Family

This plant is also a parasite. The tall leafless stalk is grooved and is covered with sticky hairs. It is brown or purple and has numerous brown scales at the base of the stem. It grows under trees or other conifers to a height up to three feet. The flowers vary from red to white and join together to form an inverted bell-shaped vase.

Indian Pipe is a parasitic plant which is usually waxy white but turns black as the fruit ripens. It is from two to twelve inches high and grows in rich, shady woods. The leaves are like white scales along the thick, fleshy stem. The single, odorless flower hangs with its own end towards the ground.

INDIAN PIPE
Monotropa uniflora
Heath Family

ONE-FLOWERED CANCER-ROOT
Orobanche uniflora
Broomrape Family

Another parasitic plant is the One-Flowered Cancer-Root which grows in damp woods. Several stems usually grow up together to a height of from two to ten inches. A single downy white or pale lavender flower is at the end of each leafless, sticky, pale-colored stalk. The pretty flower is tube-shaped and flares out into five lobes. There are two yellow bands inside on the lower side of the blossom.

PYROLA
Heath Family

The flower in center of the page shows the typical shape of all Pyrolas. They all have a circle of basal leaves and a single leafless stalk. They vary in height from six to twelve inches. Distinctive characteristics will help in identification are given for different pyrolas.

ROUND-LEAVED PYROLA

Pyrola rotundifolia is similar to Shinleaf but is larger and has leaves which are shinier and rounder. The petioles (leaf stems) are often as long as the leaf blade itself. It has white petals and grows in woods and bogs.

SHINLEAF PYROLA

Pyrola elliptica is the most common pyrola. It has large dull green elliptical leaves which are rounded at the ends. The blade of the leaf is longer than the leaf stem. Note the long curving pistils protruding from the centers of the greenish-veined white flowers.

ONE-SIDED PYROLA

Pyrola secunda. Notice how the greenish-yellow flowers are arranged on only one side of the drooping stem. The leaf blades are shining, ovate, and toothed.

GREENISH-FLOWERED PYROLA

Pyrola virens is a smaller pyrola and has thick broad leaf-blades with round ends and long stalks. The flowers are greenish and the style points downward, then turns up at the end.

WINTERGREEN or CHECKERBERRY
Gaultheria procumbens
Heath Family

Wintergreen is a low, spicy, semi-woody plant with creeping roots and underground stems. The branches are erect and upright and stand from two to six inches tall. Each stem bears several thick oblong evergreen leaves that are shiny on top and pale underneath. The flowers are white or sometimes touched with pink. They are bell-shaped and hang down from the curved stalk. They are found in woods and open places in sandy soil — especially near evergreen trees. The fruit is a bright red berry and often lasts throughout the winter until the new blossoms appear in spring.

BEARBERRY
Arctostaphylos uva-ursi
Heath Family

Bearberry is a trailing shrub with paddle-shaped evergreen leaves which forms dense carpets several yards across and only a few inches tall. It grows in sandy or rocky places and is often used as a ground-cover by highway departments.
The waxy white flowers bloom in mid-May and hang in clusters from the tips of the plant. The flowers are urn-shaped with small lobed mouth which is often touched with pink. The fruit is a dull red berry that lasts into November.

CREEPING SNOWBERRY
Gaultheria hispidula
Heath Family

This is a creeping slightly woody plant with small stiff, alternate, oval leaves and tiny bell-shaped flowers. The leaves have brownish hairs on the underside. The flowers are tiny and bell-shaped and hang singly from the leaf axils. Each flower has four lobes.

When the flowers fade, a pure white, edible berry appears. Both the fruit and the leaves have a wintergreen flavor, and last into the winter. This attractive plant grows in cold woods, bogs, and places that the sun does not hit.

57

SWAMP HONEYSUCKLE
Rhododendron viscosum
Heath Family

This is a much-branched shrub found in wet woods, swamps, and thickets. It is often as tall as six feet. The leaves are longer than wide, and the biggest part of the leaf is usually nearest to the tip of the leaf. The leaf tips can be either rounded or pointed. The trumpet-shaped white flowers have a long tube which is covered with fine, sticky, red hairs. The five long, curving stamens and the end of the pistil protrude about a half inch from the throat of the flower.

LABRADOR TEA
Ledum groenlandicum
Heath Family

This shrub grows in cold bogs and along wet shores to a height of up to three feet. The twigs are hairy and the leaves are long and narrow. The distinguishing features of this plant are the rolled-back leaves and the brown-orange wooly underside. The numerous white flowers at the top have five white petals and from five to seven stamens protruding noticeably from the center.

LOW SWEET BLUEBERRY
Vaccinium angustifolium
Heath Family

Leather-leaf is an evergreen, branching shrub which grows in bogs and forms dense thickets. It grows to a height of from one to three feet. Oblong, leather-like leaves with minutely-toothed margins alternate along the wiry stem. The stem, the underside of the leaves, and the calyx all are brown. Numerous delicate, white, bell-shaped flowers about one-fourth of an inch long hang from the base of the upturned leaves.

LEATHER-LEAF
Chamaedaphne calyculata
Heath Family

Huckleberry is a much-branched shrub that grows in dry rocky or sandy soil of thickets and woods to a height of two or three feet. The leaves are egg-shaped, untoothed, and are dotted on both sides with shining glands. The leaves are not evergreen as are the leaves on the Leather-leaf. The white bell-shaped flowers are about one-fourth of an inch long and hang in short clusters below the leaves on separate stems. The stem holding the flowers and the calyx of the flower are both hairy. The fruit is an edible black berry.

HUCKLEBERRY
Gaylussacia baccata
Heath Family

This blueberry plant is usually less than eight inches tall and grows in colonies in dry rocky or sandy soil. There are other varieties not pictured which are taller. This one is grown commercially for its bright blue berries which are raked and sold for pies and other sweets. The young stems are green and much branched, but turn brown with age. The leaves are egg-shaped, but quite pointed at the tip. They are usually smooth on both sides, though new young leaves may have a little hair along the midvein. The white corolla is cylindrical in shape and hangs in a drooping position in clusters.

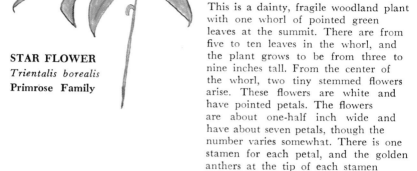

STAR FLOWER
Trientalis borealis
Primrose Family

This is a dainty, fragile woodland plant with one whorl of pointed green leaves at the summit. There are from five to ten leaves in the whorl, and the plant grows to be from three to nine inches tall. From the center of the whorl, two tiny stemmed flowers arise. These flowers are white and have pointed petals. The flowers are about one-half inch wide and have about seven petals, though the number varies somewhat. There is one stamen for each petal, and the golden anthers at the tip of each stamen are clearly visible against the white petals.

WATER PIMPERNEL
Samolus floribundus
Primrose Family

Water Pimpernel grows in ditches, muddy woods-roads, and along shores of muddy streams. It is a much-branched plant which grows to a height of from four to twelve inches. It has minute white flowers with five lobes which are in green cup-shaped calyxes which also have five lobes or teeth. (See enlargement) The leaves are alternate on the stem, but are clustered together at the base of the plant.

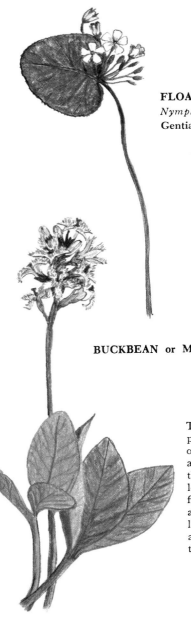

FLOATING HEARTS
Nymphoides cordatum
Gentian Family

This plant has floating water-lily-like leaves and an umbel of small white flowers. It grows in quiet water of ponds on very long, slender, submerged stems. The leaf is broadly oval with a heart-shaped base. If the plant is sterile, there is only one floating leaf, but if the plant is in bloom, there are two or more leaves. The corolla is white or cream-colored with a short tube and five petals. The calyx is parted nearly to the base and has five oblong lobes.

BUCKBEAN or MARSH TREFOIL
Menyanthes trifoliatus
Gentian Family

This plant grows in shallow water of ponds, marshes, and bogs to a height of from four to twelve inches. It has a stout stem with alternate leaves near the base. Each leaf has three oval leaflets. The white, funnel-shaped flower has five recurved petals which are fringed on the inner surface with long white hairs. The flowers are in a tight terminal cluster at the end of the stem.

61

WHITE MILKWEED
Asclepias variegata
Milkweed Family

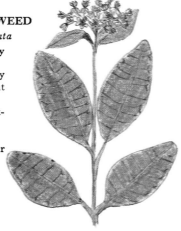

White Milkweed grows in moist or dry upland woods and thickets to a height of from two to three feet. The stout stem has several pairs of oblong, blunt-tipped leaves. The flowers are white with purplish centers and are in a terminal cluster. The flower is similar to that of most milkweeds (see page 112 for enlargement), but the five cups above the five turned-back petals are rounded outward on this milkweed.

POKE MILKWEED
Asclepias exaltata
Milkweed Family

Poke Milkweed is from three to six feet tall and grows in the moist upland woods. It has thin leaves which have broad middles but are pointed at each end. The leaves are often in a drooping position. The flower is white to dull-purple and the hoods are white to pink. They are arranged in several loosely-flowered umbels which are in a drooping position from the upper leaf axils.

WHORLED MILKWEED
Asclepias verticillata
Milkweed Family

This milkweed grows in dry or moist fields, along roads, and in upland woods. It generally has an unbranched stem which is from one to two feet tall. The leaves are very slender and the edges are rolled underneath. There are from three to six leaves in circles around the stem at regular intervals. The flowers are like typical milkweed flowers, but are smaller. They are greenish-white and are in clusters at the leaf axils.

Wild Potato-Vine is a long trailing and twining plant similar to the garden-grown Morning Glories. It has a large funnel-shaped white flower with pink stripes reaching out from the center. The leaves are very heart-shaped and each leaf is attached to the main stem individually. It is found in dry fields and roadsides.

WILD POTATO-VINE
Ipomoca pandurata
Morning-Glory Family

HEDGE BINDWEED
Convolvulus sepium
Morning-Glory Family

This is a white flower, but see the pink section, page 114 for a detailed description of Bindweed.

FIELD BINDWEED
Convolvulus arvensis
Morning-Glory Family

Field Bindweed is very similar to Hedge Bindweed, but the leaves are much smaller and less pointed at the tips. The flowers are less than an inch wide and vary from white to pink, but are usually white. This wild flower is widespread throughout New England and grows prostrate along the ground or climbs over shrubs, stonewalls, compost heaps, and decaying boxes and buildings.

63

BROAD-LEAVED WATERLEAF
Hydrophyllum canadense
Waterleaf Family

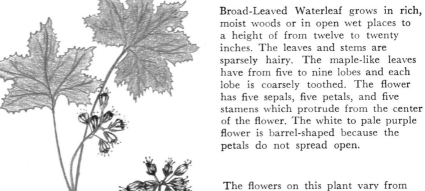

Broad-Leaved Waterleaf grows in rich, moist woods or in open wet places to a height of from twelve to twenty inches. The leaves and stems are sparsely hairy. The maple-like leaves have from five to nine lobes and each lobe is coarsely toothed. The flower has five sepals, five petals, and five stamens which protrude from the center of the flower. The white to pale purple flower is barrel-shaped because the petals do not spread open.

The flowers on this plant vary from white to pale violet. Look on page 122 in the violet section for details about this plant.

VIRGINIA WATERLEAF
Hydrophyllum virginianum
Waterleaf Family

Jimsonweed is a coarse upright weed of fields, barnyards, and waste places. The plant is poisonous. The flowers are white to lavender and trumpet-shaped usually — from three to five inches long. The green cup-like calyx tube is half as long as the flower itself.
The leaves are very thin, pointed at the tip, and are deeply cut with uneven triangular teeth. Each leaf is singly attached to the main stem.
In some species of Jimsonweed, the stem is green and the flowers are white; another species has a purple stem and pale violet blossoms.

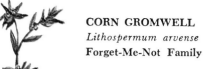

CORN GROMWELL
Lithospermum arvense
Forget-Me-Not Family

This rough, hairy plant grows from a
slender taproot, but is often branched
at the base. It grows in waste places
to a height of from twelve to thirty
inches. It has small, stemless, five-
petaled white flowers tucked among the
leafy bracts in the axils of the upper
leaves. The calyx lobes are nearly as
long as the white petals. The long,
narrow, oval leaves alternate along the
stem.

This plant grows in dry open places
and on rocky banks to a height of
from three to fifteen inches. The erect
stems are branching from a common
base and often begin to flower when
they are less than four inches tall. The
stems lengthen as more buds open.
The linear to oblong leaves are alternate
on the hairy stems. The white, tubular
flowers have five lobes and are less
than one-sixth of an inch broad. The
five calyx lobes are bristly and unequal.

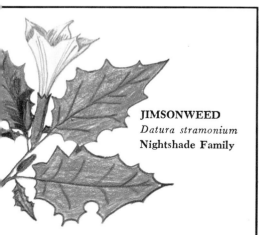

JIMSONWEED
Datura stramonium
Nightshade Family

**SPRING FORGET-ME-NOT or
SPRING SCORPION-GRASS**
Myosotis virginica
Forget-Me-Not Family

65

CULVER'S ROOT
Veronicastrum virginicum
Snapdragon Family

Culver's Root grows in moist or dry upland woods and thickets to a height of from three to seven feet. It has slender, pointed leaves in whorls of three or six. The white flowers are tubular with four or five lobes. Two stamens and the style protrude from the throat of the flower giving the crowded flower-spike a fuzzy appearance.

MOTH MULLEIN
Verbascum blattaria
Snapdragon Family

This plant grows as a weed along roadsides, in vacant lots and other waste places to a height of from one to three feet. The stem is slender and fuzzy and the leaves vary in size and shape. They are lance-shaped in general outline and are coarsely toothed and covered with whitish wool. The flat, five-lobed flowers may be either white or yellow and are on separate pedicels (flower stems) at the top of the plant. The buds are roundish and button-like.

WHITE MULLEIN
Verbascum lychnitis
Snapdragon Family

This mullein grows along roads and in sandy fields and waste lands to a height up to four feet. The stem is branched and the plant is covered with white wool. The flowers are smaller than those on Moth Mullein, and may be either white or yellow. The flowers have five lobes and are arranged in a branching pyramid-shaped cluster at the top of the plant.

PURSLANE SPEEDWELL
Veronica peregrina
Snapdragon Family

This smooth, juicy plant grows in waste areas, along roadsides, and in cultivated grounds to a height of from three to fifteen inches. The lower leaves are paired and sometimes toothed, but the leaves on the upper extensions of the stem are alternate and untoothed. The tiny white flowers are one-twelfth of an inch broad and are tucked singly in the leaf axils. There are four petals and the bottom one is smaller than the other three. The green calyx is almost as large as the white corolla.

EYEBRIGHT
Euphrasia americana
Snapdragon Family

Eyebright grows in fields and roadsides to a height of less than a foot. It has tiny paired leaves with from three to five sharp points on each side margin. The flowers grow from the axils of the leaves and have practically no stem. They have a four-lobed calyx and a two-lipped corolla. The bottom lip is lobed. The upper lip is pale blue or lavender and the bottom lip is white with violet lines.

NORTHERN BEDSTRAW
Galium boreale
Bedstraw Family

Northern Bedstraw grows in rocky
meadows, on shores, or along streams
to a height of from twelve to forty
inches. It has linear leaves in whorls
of four around the stem. Each leaf
has three nerves on it. Numerous tiny,
white, four-petaled flowers are in tight
compound clusters. The stems are
smooth and sparsely branched below
the flower clusters.

FRAGRANT BEDSTRAW or
SWEET-SCENTED BEDSTRAW
Galium triflorum
Bedstraw Family

This bedstraw grows in woods and
thickets and reclines on nearby plants.
It has narrow lance-shaped leaves in
whorls of six at regular intervals on the
stem. The upper leaves have a minute
spine at the tip, and the leaf margins
are rough or scratchy to touch. The
greenish flowers (or burs which follow
the flowers) are in sets of threes at
the end of the branches and from axils
of leaves.

WHITE WILD LICORICE
Galium circaezans
Bedstraw Family

Wild Licorice grows in rich dry woods to a height of from one to two feet. It may be either simple or branching from the base. It has somewhat hairy stems with whorls of four broad oval leaves with from three to five nerves in them. The tiny greenish-white flowers are in few-flowered clusters on slender forked stalks at the top part of the plant.

WILD MADDER
Galium mollugo
Bedstraw Family

Wild Madder is similar to the other bedstraws, but has narrow leaves in circles of eight around the stem. The leaves are wider at the tip than in the middle. It is a smooth, erect plant which grows in fields and along roads to a height of twelve to forty inches. The base is often lying on the ground, and where many plants grow together, a mat will form at the base of the upright stems. Numerous minute, white flowers are in tight clusters at the top of the plant.

Hobblebush is a straggling, woody bush as tall as six or eight feet which grows in damp woods. The tips of the lower, arching branches often touch the ground and take root. These arching branches which are rooted at both ends often make it difficult for people trying to pass by. The young stems, buds, and leaf veins are covered with rusty-colored wooly hairs. The opposite leaves are very broad and are either round or heart-shaped. The large leaves may be up to six inches across and are irregularly toothed at the margins. The flowers appear in mid-May and are in white flat-topped clusters. The showy outer flowers are much larger than the inside flowers, but they have no reproductive parts in them. The fruit is bright red, but turns purple. It is arranged in large, loose umbrella-like clusters.

HOBBLEBUSH
Viburnum alnifolium
Honeysuckle Family

This arching shrub grows to heights of fifteen or more feet in rich shade woodlands. The leaves are opposite and are divided into either five or seven pointed leaflets with toothed margins. The small white flowers are arranged in rounded clusters. The flowers open in May, but the shrub becomes more conspicuous as the pyramid-shaped clusters of berries turn scarlet. These berries are not edible as are the flat-topped clusters of purple-black berries of the American Elder.

RED-BERRIED ELDER
Sambucus pubens
Honeysuckle Family

YARROW
Achillea millefolium
Composite Family

Yarrow is a wooly plant with soft aromatic, fern-like leaves and a flat-topped, or rounded flower cluster. Close inspection seems to reveal single five-petaled flowers — but this is not true. These are really flower heads and the five "petals" are five ray flowers, each of which is a complete flower in itself. The flower-cluster is usually white but is rarely pink. Yarrow grows along roadsides and in fields to a height of from one to three feet.

FIELD PUSSYTOES
Antennaria neglecta
Composite Family

This smaller Pussytoes spreads by long slender runners and often forms dense mats in dry fields and open slopes. The basal leaves have only one main rib and they are spoon-shaped. They taper as they near the stem. The flower stem is from four to twelve inches tall, has several very narrow stem leaves, and several crowded flower heads at the top. The crowded heads pressed closely together form a rounded, knobbed cluster like a kitten's paw.

LANTAIN-LEAVED PUSSYTOES
ntennaria plantaginifolia
omposite Family

This plant is from three to sixteen inches tall and grows in dry soil in woods and pastures. The leaves are mostly at the base. Basal leaves have long stalks and are spoon-shaped with from three to five lengthwise veins. The leaves are silky and the stem is wooly. The stem leaves are much smaller and are lance-shaped and scale-like. There are several flower heads in a cluster at the top. These have white and purplish hairs and bracts below each head. The bracts are usually white-tipped.

71

This daisy-like plant grows abundantly in waste places and in barnyards to a height of from eight to twenty-four inches. The foliage is thrice-cut and has a very strong unpleasant odor. The leaves also cause blisters on hands of farm workers who harvest this along with the hay crop. Other names are Stinking Chamomile and Dog-Fennel.

STINKING MAYWEED
Anthemis cotula
Composite Family

Daisy Fleabane is a coarse aster-like flower which grows in fields and wastelands to a height of from one to five feet. It blooms very early in the spring and the true asters bloom later. This plant has a single circle of bracts under the flower head. They do not overlap each other as they do on the aster. The plant is very hairy and has numerous strongly-toothed leaves.

DAISY FLEABANE
Erigeron annuus
Composite Family

OX-EYE DAISY
Chrysanthemum leucanthemum
Composite Family

This familiar plant grows abundantly in fields and along roadsides. It has dark narrow, much-lobed leaves and is from one to three feet tall. What appears to be a single flower with white petals is really a group of very tiny flowers of two types. The disk flowers are yellow and in the center, but are too numerous and too small to be seen without a magnifying glass. The ray flowers are the white petal-shaped rays that grow outward around the yellow center.

WILD CHAMOMILE
Matricaria chamomilla
Composite Family

Wild Chamomile is a branching
pineapple-scented weed which grows in
waste places and along roadsides to
a height of eight to thirty-two inches.
The leaves are finely cut into linear
segments. The numerous daisy-like heads
have yellow centers and white rays
which have five teeth at the tips.

FEVERFEW
Chrysanthemum parthenium
Composite Family

Corn-marigold is another name for this
flower. It grows in waste places to a
height of from twelve to thirty-two
inches. It is a bushy plant with a
pungent aroma and deeply-lobed gray-
green leaves. It has many daisy-like
flower heads with large yellow centers
and short, stubby white rays.

GALLANT SOLDIERS
Galinsoga parviflora
Composite Family

This weed grows in waste places and
around old dwellings to a height of
from six to eighteen inches. There are
hairs lying flat on the surface of the
stem. The tiny inconspicuous flower
heads are about one-fourth of an inch
across. The conical center is orange-
yellow and there are four or five white
rays — each of which has three lobes
at the tip. The broad leaves are
coarsely toothed and the lower leaves
are on petioles (leaf stems).
The plant and flowers are so tiny an
enlargement has been made to show
detail.

73

Field Garlic grows in fields and
meadows to a height of from one to
three feet. The "head" contains
pink or white flowers mixed with
bulblets with tails. These tails are
really a long fragile leaf.
There is a single papery bract below
the umbel of flowers. This plant
has very slender rounded leaves which
ascend part way up the stem.
The leaves are not flat like grass,
but are rounded. They are usually
hollow towards the base of the leaf.

This plant has a strong onion-like
odor. It grows in moist meadows
or open woods to a height of from
ten to twenty-four inches. The stem
is erect and is leafy only on the lower
third of the plant. The leaves are
flat and narrow like grass. They are
not hollow as in the field species.
The umbel at the top of the stem
differs from plant to plant.
There are many bulblets in the group
Usually there are two or three pink
or white flowers, but this is not
always the case. There is a spathe
under the umbel which has three
parts — unlike the one-part spathe
in the field species.
Another common name for this plant
is Wild Garlic.

FIELD GARLIC
Allium vineale
Lily Family

MEADOW GARLIC
Allium canadense
Lily Family

The two flowers on the opposite page
are combined, not because they are in
the same family or are related in any
way, but because they are both found
on remote, rocky, off-shore ledges
or on coastal islands.

ROSEROOT
SEDUM
Sedum rosea
Sedum Family

WILD CHIVES
Allium
schoenoprasum
var. sibricium
Lily Family

This tall plant emits a very strong onion-like odor. At the base of the stout stem is a whitish bulb which is often narrower than the stem itself. The leaves are erect and hollow, often turning brown and hanging down as the flower head matures.
The numerous flowers are arranged in a compact head at the top.
Each flower is bell-shaped and points upward on its own tiny pedicel.
There are six pointed, pink or lavender petals with a whitish base and a fine purple line at the midrib of each petal. Below the flower cluster are two wide, papery bracts which look very much like the outside skin on an onion.

This is an arctic plant which is found growing in large clumps in depressions of rock ledges on off-shore islands of Maine, and in higher elevations further south. It has a thick, juicy, light-colored stem which emits the odor of roses when crushed.
The pale-green leaves are usually tipped with red, are about an inch long, and have teeth at the tips. The leaves are crowded, arranged in circles, and overlap each other spirally. The flowers are at the summit of the stem in a flat-topped, circular cluster. There are separate male and female flowers on each plant. The male flowers are yellowish and the female flowers are reddish or purplish. After fertilization, the female flower develops into a four-beaked, dry cluster. The top of each looks like a four-pointed, orange star and this changes the flat-topped flower cluster from red to bright orange.

75

PINK MANDARIN or
ROSE TWISTED STALK
Streptopus roseus
Lily Family

The Twisted Stalk has sharply-pointed leaves arranged alternately along a zigzag forked stem. The flowers are bell-shaped and about one-half inch long. They have six pointed pink or purplish petals which curve upwards only at the tips.

The flowers do not hang from the axils of the leaf as in most plants, but grow from the side of the stem opposite the leaf. The flower stalk then doubles back so that the flower hangs beneath the leaf.

Another Twisted Stalk is on page 175 in the white section.

The trillium is an early spring flower which often blooms before the first robin has returned from the warm south. There are many kinds of trilliums, but all have the same general structure based on three. The trilliums have three leaves, three petals, three sepals, a three-part pistil, and six stamens.

Red Trillium has an unpleasant odor and is often called Stinking Benjamin or Ill-Scented Wake-Robin.

It grows in woods to a height of seven to twenty-four inches. The leaves vary greatly in size and are below the flower. The flower has petals which are over an inch long.

In Canada, people thought that if someone was bitten by a rattlesnake and chewed the root of this plant, they would get well. The root tastes terrible and is very sickening, but some people use it as a medicine.

RED TRILLIUM
or WAKE-ROBIN
Trillium erectum
Lily Family

GRASS-PINK or CALOPOGON
Calopogon pulchellus
Orchid Family

This orchid appears to be "upside down" as the yellow, crested lip is upright at the top whereas in most other orchids the crested, hairy lip is at the bottom. This orchid grows in wet acid soil of bogs, peat meadows, and swamps to a height of from four to eighteen inches. The slender grass-like stem has from two to ten orchids at the top and a single, slender leaf which sheaths the stem at the base. Both the stalk and the leaf grow from a very small white bulb. The flowers are rose-purple to pink and are from one to one and three-fourths inches long.

ROSE POGONIA
or SNAKE-MOUTH
Pogonia ophioglossoides
Orchid Family

Rose Pogonia grows in acid soil of wet meadows and sphagnum bogs to a height of from eight to sixteen inches. Each plant has perfumed flowers singly — or in a pair — at the summit of the stem. There is a single broad leaf sheathing the stem at mid-point. The color range is from pale lavender to bright rose and rarely white. The petals and sepals are about the same size and have a silky texture. The showy, fringed lower lip is crested with yellow hairs.

DRAGON'S MOUTH
or ARETHUSA
Arethusa bulbosa
Orchid Family

This is a shorter-stemmed orchid than the two preceding ones. It grows to a height of from five to ten inches, is usually in groups of several, and grows best in sphagnum bogs, swamps, or mossy depressions in moist woods. The single flower at the top is from one to two inches high. The three erect sepals and the two hood-like petals are above the drooping lip. The lip is variegated with purplish blotches and is crested down the face with three hairy ridges. There are from one to three loose bracts toward the base. After the flower dies, a single grass-like leaf will grow from within the upper bract.

Here are four members of the orchid family which are becoming more and more rare in New England. It would be wise to enjoy these flowers without picking them to insure their availability for the enjoyment of future generations.

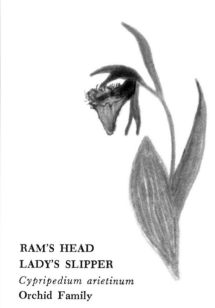

RAM'S HEAD
LADY'S SLIPPER
Cypripedium arietinum
Orchid Family

This orchid has from three to four wide veined leaves on the stem and is from six to twelve inches tall. Two of the petals are greenish brown and very narrow. They look like shoelaces above the shoe. The third petal forms an inflated pouch which is white but veined with crimson. It is lined with silky white hairs. The tip is elongated into a blunt spur that gives the "ram's head" look to the flower.

This orchid has two oval leaves which are from six to eight inches long. They grow from the base of the flower stalk. Each plant has only one stem and one flower. One pink petal is puffed out to look like the toe of a slipper. This petal is delicately veined with purple. The slipper may be as long as two inches on a healthy plant. The brownish "shoelaces" at the top add to the shoe-like appearances.

MOCCASIN FLOWER or PINK LADY'S SLIPPER
Cypripedium acaule
Orchid Family

SHOWY ORCHIS
Orchis spectabilis
Orchid Family

SHOWY LADY'S SLIPPER
Cypripedium reginae
Orchid Family
See page 16 for detailed description.

The showy orchis has two wide, smooth basal leaves and is from four to ten inches high. It usually has from three to eight flowers which are about an inch long. The arching hood is rose-lavender and the bottom lipped petal and spur are white. It grows in rich woods and is more common than the Showy Lady's Slipper.

LARGE PURPLE FRINGED ORCHID
Habenaria psycodes var. grandiflora
Orchid Family

This orchid has many rose-purple or
lavender to pink flowers in a
cylindrical cluster at the top of the
stalk. It has large lower leaves which
are oval at the base and pointed at
the tip, and upper leaves which are
small and linear. The orchid grows in
woods and meadows to a height of
from one to five feet. The sepals are
oval and the petals are spatulate shape
and are finely toothed. The lip is
deeply three-parted and each lobe is
fan-shaped, and so deeply toothed th
it appears to be fringed. The lip is
up to three-fourths of an inch long.
There is a tubular, hollow spur whic
extends backwards or downwards
from the base of the flower.

FAIRY SLIPPER
or CALYPSO
Calypso bulbosa
Orchid Family

This lovely little orchid grows in deep,
mossy, coniferous woods to a height
of from four to eight inches. The
Fairy Slipper produces a single round-
oval basal leaf in the fall which lasts
through to flowering time. In the
spring, the underground bulb sends up a
leafless scape (flowering stem directly
from the ground), which bears a
solitary flower at the top. The flow
is similar in shape to a lady slipper
and is about three-fourths of an inc
long. The sepals and side petals are
similar in shape and are pale purple.
The boat-shaped lip is whitish and
shades to yellow toward the tip. It h
reddish-brown or purple-brown marks
on the inside. The lip is spotted with
purple and is crested with three row
of yellow hairs. There are two tiny
horns at the toe of the slipper. This
rare orchid (Calypso) should never
be picked.

LARGE TWAYBLADE
Liparis lilifolia
Orchid Family

This orchid has two broad, elliptical
basal leaves and many dull, mauve —
almost brownish at times — flowers
with very broad lips. The narrow
lateral petals are greenish to pale purple
and are usually rolled and twisted
under the lip. The pale-purple lip is
flat and broad. The sepals are greenish
white. This orchid grows in rich,
mossy woods or ravines to a height of
from four to twelve inches.

81

SMARTWEED or PINKWEED
Polygonum pensylvanicum
Buckwheat Family

There are many smartweeds in our
area. They are all attractive plants
with "spikes" of variegated pink and
white flowers. The pictured species is a
branched weed in fields, waste places
and along roadsides. It is from one to
four feet high. The sheaths around
the leaf axils are *not fringed*. The
joints are reddish and the long pointed
leaves are shiny. The cylindrical
"spikes" of flowers are dense, erect,
and blunt at the top. They are generally
bright pink, but occasionally are white.

KNOTWEED
Polygonum prolificum
Buckwheat Family

There are many different species of
knotweeds in our area. They are small,
tiny-leaved plants with insignificant
flowers tucked in the leaf axils. The
minute flowers are either single, in
pairs, or in sets of three. The variety
shown is a coastal variety, but also grows
inland. The leaves get very veiny
when dry, and the flowers can scarcely
be seen.

LADY'S THUMB or REDLEG
Polygonum persicaria
Buckwheat Family

This plant is similar to Smartweed,
but the papery sheaths at the base of
the leaves are *fringed* with bristles. The
pink flower spike is dense, but rarely
more than an inch long. The leaves
often have a dark, triangular-shaped
blotch in the center. The stems are
reddish.

ARROW-LEAVED TEARTHUMB
Polygonum sagittatum
Buckwheat Family

This slender-stemmed plant grows in
marshes and in wet meadows to a
height of from two to six feet. Usually
it rests on the tops of other plants.
The stem and the bottom side of the
leaf midrib have hooked sharp prickles.
The leaves are long, narrow, and
arrow-head shaped. The flowers are
either pink or white and are in very
small clusters.

CAROLINA
SPRING BEAUTY
Claytonia caroliniana
Purslane Family

This Wide-Leaved Spring Beauty is
very similar to the one at the left but l
wider leaves with short leaf stems
(petioles). The flowers are a little
smaller and are usually white with pi
veins.

VIRGINIA
SPRING BEAUTY
Claytonia virginica
Purslane Family

This spring flower can be found in
thick carpet-like masses blooming in
moist open woods during April and
May. It is from four to twelve inches
tall and has shiny, grass-like leaves
which are opposite each other on the
stem. The stems are often lying on the
ground instead of standing erect. The
flower stalks end in clusters of pink
blossoms with dark pink veins. Each
flower is five-petaled and when fully
opened may measure an inch across. The
average blossom, however, is usually
about one-half inch. The whole plant
is frail, and if picked, the blossoms will
close and the entire plant will wilt
unless placed in water very soon. The
blossoms are so fragile, they close tightly
if the weather turns cold or if
the sky becomes cloudy.

WILD PINK
Silene caroliniana
Pink Family

Wild Pink forms a short thick mass
slender leaves and five-petaled flowe
and grows in dry sandy or rocky ope
woods. The upper stems and calyx
are often sticky. The stems are up
to eight inches tall with oblong lea
well separated and up to two inches
long. The flowers are usually cluster
above the tuft of leaves at the bas
Each flower has wedge-shaped pink
petals and darker eyes at the center.

DEPTFORD PINK
Dianthus armeria
Pink Family

This is a slender stiff plant with needle-like leaves which stand up close to the plant. It grows in dry fields and in waste places to a height of from eight inches to three feet. At the tip of the plant are one or more tight clusters of small flowers and buds which usually open one at a time. Each cluster has a pair of long leaf bracts and each individual blossom has a single bract beneath it. The flower has five rose-colored petals with toothed edges and tiny white spots on it.

EEPY
TCHFLY
ene
irrhina
k Family

This plant is easily recognized by the dark sticky places mid-way between each pair of leaves. The stem is from eight to thirty inches tall and the pairs of narrow leaves are spaced wide apart. Below the tiny pink or white flowers there is an inflated bladder. On some plants, the petals are not present.

RAGGED-ROBIN
Lychnis flos-cuculi
Pink Family

This member of the pink family is quickly identified by its four deeply cleft rose or white petals. The plant is from one to three feet tall and grows in fields and wet meadows where it often covers large areas.

The Fire Pink is one of our most vivid spring wild flowers. Its deep crimson blossoms may be found in dry, open woods from May to August. It is so attractive that people often cultivate it in rock gardens or wild flower gardens.

The Fire Pink grows to a height of one to two feet. The dark green leaves around the base of the plant are long and thin and are narrowed from the tip to the base.

The stems and leaves are covered with little hairs. These hairs give off a sticky fluid which makes the plant sticky to touch. Insects often have difficulty climbing on this plant an often get their feet so gummed up th die. For this reason, it is often calle *Catchfly*.

This wildflower belongs to the pink family. It has five deep crimson oblo petals which are notched at the tip. Its ten stamens may be seen protruding from the throat of the flow The flowers are about one inch in diameter and are loosely clustered together at the end of the flower sta

FIRE PINK
Silene virginica
Pink Family

WILD COLUMBINE
Aquilegia canadensis
Buttercup Family

This wild flower is one of the most beautiful, delicate, and odd-shaped of our New England wild flowers. The name columbine comes from a Latin word "columba" which means dove. Some people think the petals resemble doves. The flower on the Wild Columbine looks like a ballet skirt of gold and scarlet. Each flower has five petals which seem to grow backwards from the stems. The flowers hang downward from the stem instead of facing up. The stamens of this flower hang down below the petals and give a jewel-like effect. There are other species of columbine which may be white, purple, or blue, but those which are most common in New England are red with yellow centers. The plant itself grows to a height of one to two feet. It grows in rocky woods and slopes and amid boulders on shady wooded banks. For this reason, some call this wild flower Rock Bells. The leaves of the columbine seem to grow at the bottom of the plant and the flowers tower above them. Each leaf is divided into three parts and each part is re-divided into sets of three scalloped leaflets.

This vine is found on moist wooded slopes or rocky, shaded cliffs. It climbs over bushes and supports itself by its coiling leafstalks. The leaves are divided into many small, round, toothed segments usually in sets of three. The main stalk may climb to a height of from ten to twelve feet. The flowers hang in drooping clusters from leaf axils and are whitish or pale pink. Each flower has four petals which are united into a hollow corolla about one-half of an inch long.

ALLEGHENY-VINE or
CLIMBING FUMITORY

Adlumia fungosa
Poppy Family

FUMITORY
or EARTH-SMOKE
Fumaria officinalis
Poppy Family

Fumitory is a gray-green climbing plant with finely cut leaflets in sets of three or five. The stem is very lax and much branched and is from eight to forty inches long. The finely pronged leaflets are a gray-green color and give the appearance of smoke from a distance. The flowers are in racemes and are pinkish purple and tipped with maroon. The summit is sometimes dark red. Each flower has a single spur and is about one and one-half inches long.

TWO-LEAVED TOOTHWORT
or CRINKLEROOT
Dentaria diphylla
Mustard Family

The Two-Leaved Toothwort grows in rich, moist woods and thickets to a height of from eight to fourteen inches. It has a rather thick, smooth stem and two leaves midway on the stem. The leaves are notched or toothed and are divided into three parts. There are other leaves arising on long stems from the base of the plant. The flowers are white or pinkish-white and are found in a loose cluster at the end of the stem. Each blossom has four cross-like petals. The green cup-like sepals are very noticeable on the back of the flower. The root is wrinkled and toothed. It is edible and tastes similar to watercress.

PALE CORYDALIS
Corydalis sempervirens
Poppy Family

This slender-stemmed, erect plant is found in dry rocky woods and grows to a height of from one to two feet. The leaves are deeply cut and are grayish green in color. The leaves are often covered with a white powdery substance. The lower leaves have leaf stems (petioles) but the upper leaves are attached directly to the main stem. The flowers are arranged in branching groups and each one has a pale pink single bulbous spur with yellow lips.

CUT-LEAVED
TOOTHWORT
Dentaria laciniata
Mustard Family

This favorite spring flower grows in rich moist woods to a height of from eight to fifteen inches. There is a whorl of three leaves part way up on the stem. These are three-parted nearly to the base and each part is deeply toothed. The flowers are about one-half to three-fourths of an inch wide and are fragrant. They vary from white, to pink, to pale purple and are gathered together at the top of the stem. As the flowers fade, seed pods which are about an inch long appear.

DAME'S ROCKET
Hesperis matronalis
Mustard Family

This plant is also known as Dame's Violet and Mother-of-the-Evening. It is a tall plant — sometimes three feet or more — which grows along roadside and in open woods. The leaves are pointed, toothed, and attached to th stem with a short stalk (petiole). The beautiful, four-petaled blossoms are up to an inch across and vary from white through pink to purple. The flowers at the bottom open first, and as seed pods form, the top part of the stem lengthens so other buds ma have room to open. The seed pods are very narrow and may be as lon as five inches when they are mature.

PURPLE CRESS
Cardamine douglassii
Mustard Family

This is a much smaller plant than the Dame's Rocket, but both are members of the same family. Purple Cress grows in wet woods and near springs to a height of from five to twelve inches. The stem is hairy an the basal leaves are round and have long stalks. The stem leaves do not have stalks, but are attached directl to the main stem. Stem leaves are long and toothed, not round as the basal leaves are. The flowers have four pin petals with yellow stamens protruding from the center. The buds are clustere together at the top of the stem, and only a few flowers open at a time, the bottom buds opening first.

WILD GINGER
Asarum canadense
Birthwort Family

PITCHER-PLANT
Sarracenia purpurea
Pitcher-Plant Family

This odd-looking plant bears only one cup-shaped deep-red flower in the crotch of the two leaf stalks. The flower has three pointed lobes and twelve stamens. It lies close to, or on, the ground so small early flies and insects, which keep close to the ground, can spread the pollen to develop the seed. Wild Ginger grows in rich woods and is from six to twelve inches tall. The two heart-shaped leaves grow on long leaf stems from the base of the plant. The leaves are thick and softly fuzzy and are beautifully veined. The top of the leaf is deep green and the underside is usually lighter in color. Because the flower is often hidden in decaying leaves of the forest floor, the leaves are actually the most showy part of the plant. The root is used as a spice, for medicinal purposes, and as a candied sweet.

Another odd-looking plant is the Pitcher-Plant. It has hollow pitcher-like leaves which are from four to twelve inches long and are usually half filled with water. The leaves are heavily veined and the spreading rim of the leaf is lined with downward-pointing hairs. The leaves trap insects which enter and the plant then digests the soft parts of the insects. The insects also furnish food for larvae of flies which help to cross-pollinate the flowers. The single rose-purple flower is about two inches broad and hangs down from the flower stalk which is from one to two feet high. There are five spreading greenish sepals and five purple petals which curve inward to inclose the flattened yellow center and the umbrella-like stigma. Pitcher-Plants grow in sphagnum bogs.

NORTHEASTERN ROSE
Rosa nitida
Rose Family

This low slender shrub is found in swamps, bogs, or in moist soil. It grows to a height of from one to three feet. The stem has many slender, straight, dark purple bristles which are all about the same length. The flower is pink and about two inches broad. The leaf has many small crowded leaflets.

SWEETBRIER
Rosa eglanteria
Rose Family

A distinguishing feature of this plant is the stout thorns which curve downward. The long arching stems have many pink flowers which are smaller than most other roses. The leaves are more round than most roses and are double toothed — a smaller tooth between each two larger teeth.

PASTURE ROSE
Rosa carolina
Rose Family

This rose is found in dry rocky ground and upland pastures and grows to a height of from six inches to three feet. It is a much-branched shrub. The flowers are two inches broad and have a delightful aroma. A distinctive characteristic is the sharp slender straight thorns which grow only where the leaves branch off from the stems.

PURPLE-FLOWERING
RASPBERRY
Rubus odoratus
Rose Family

This shrub grows in shady rocky woods
or moist ravines. It has maple-shaped
leaves which are from five to ten inches
broad. The leaves and the stem are
both hairy. The stem does not have
prickly spines as do other raspberries.
On older, larger stems the bark sheds.
The five-petaled flower is similar to
that of a rose. It is purplish red in
color and about two inches across. It
has broad, long, brown sepals. After
the flower fades, a dry acid berry
develops.

RUGOSA ROSE
or WRINKLED ROSE
Rosa rugosa
Rose Family

This rose has very large deep rose
blossoms which sometimes fade to
white. It is a large shrub of sand dunes,
seasides, and roadsides which grows
to a height of from two to six feet.
The distinctive characteristic is the
heavily wrinkled leaves and the bristly
stems. The stem and the thorns
themselves are hairy.

This cinquefoil has reclining or erect reddish-green stems that rise from a long underground stem. The large leaves are on long petioles and have from five to seven toothed leaflets. The three leaflets at the end of the petiole are united. There are only a few flowers at the top of the leafy, hairy stem. The flowers are a deep red-purple and the five petals are shorter and narrower than the wide, purple sepals. The plant is from eight to twenty-four inches tall.

MARSH CINQUEFOIL
Potentilla palustris
Rose Family

CROWN VETCH
Coronilla varia
Pea Family

This Vetch is similar to other vetche except for the circle of white and p bi-colored flowers in a crown or circle at the top of the creeping stem The leaves have many paired, small leaflets. See page 191 for description of other vetches.

EUROPEAN GREAT BURNET
Sanguisorba officinalis
Rose Family

This plant is from ten to twenty inches tall and grows in wet places and low fields. It is not native to America and has escaped from cultivation. The flowers have four purple-brown sepals which look like petals. They are tightly compacted on a football-shaped spike which is from one-half to one and one-fou inches long. The leaves have many pairs of spade-shaped leaflets with teeth on the edges.

Beach Pea is a stout, reclining plant with branching stems as long as four and five feet. It grows along sea beaches and lake shores. The main stems and the leaf-bearing stems are sharply angled with four flat sides, but the part of the stem which bears the flowers is round. The leaflets are pea-green in color and are usually in pairs. There is a sharp point at the tip of the otherwise toothless leaflet. There are large arrowhead-shaped stipules which embrace the stalk at the point where new branches occur. The flowers are in long-stalked clusters of from three to ten. They vary in color from pink to purple and are about three-fourths of an inch long. They are shaped like sweet peas and the lower lip is lighter in color than the turned-back upper lip.

BEACH PEA
Lathyrus japonicus
or *Lathyrus maritimus*
Pea Family

MARSH PEA or VETCHLING
Lathyrus palustris
Pea Family

This Marsh Pea can be distinguished from Beach Pea (described above) by the wide, flat wing on each side of the stem. The bracts at leaf axils are not the large, arrowhead shape as on Beach Pea, but look like two triangles joined together on each side of the stem. Marsh Pea grows in meadows and marshes and along the shores.

SPRING VETCH
or TARE
Vicia sativa
Pea Family

This plant is similar to Blue Vetch on page 191 but has pairs of wedge-shaped leaflets with a notch at the square tip. The flowers can be pink or purple, and are either in pairs or solitary in the leaf axils. It grows from one to three feet high in meadows and along roads.

RED CLOVER
Trifolium pratense
Pea Family

The magenta and white round head of the Red Clover is familiar to all. Red Clover grows from six to thirty inches tall in fields and along paths and roads. The stem is covered with soft white hairs. The leaf has three parts, and each leaflet has a lighter green triangular shape in the middle. There is a light green, papery sheath on the stem from which new leaves grow. A close look at a freshly-opened head is a great reward. The points on the round head are actually perfect sweet-pea-like flowers with a magenta upper hood and a white three-lobed bottom lip.

RABBIT'S FOOT CLOVER
Trifolium arvense
Pea Family

This clover is easy to identify by its fuzzy, grayish-pink, cylindrical heads. The leaves are parted into three narrow segments. Rabbit's Foot Clover grows in waste places and along roadsides to a height of from four to sixteen inches.

ALSIKE CLOVER
Trifolium hybridum
Pea Family

ALFALFA
Medicago sativa
Pea Family

This fragile plant grows in open woods and fields to a height of from four to eight inches. The stems are brownish and the leaves have three inverted, heart-shaped leaflets which often fold along the center crease. On this species of oxalis, the center point and the underside of the leaves are reddish or purplish. There are several flaring flowers on each stem. The five petals are rose-purple to violet and the "eye" is yellow-green with fine purple veins. The seed pods split open with force and scatter seeds in all directions.

VIOLET WOOD-SORREL
Oxalis violacea
Wood-Sorrel Family

COMMON WOOD-SORREL
Oxalis montana
Wood-Sorrel Family

Very similar to the above species is this common Wood-Sorrel. The flowers are borne singly on stalks from three to six inches long. The petals are white or pale pink and are marked with pink veins. Sometimes the tips of the petals are deeply notched. The leaves are similar to the one above, but are not red on the bottom.

See page 45 in the white section for details.

See page 191 in the blue section for details.

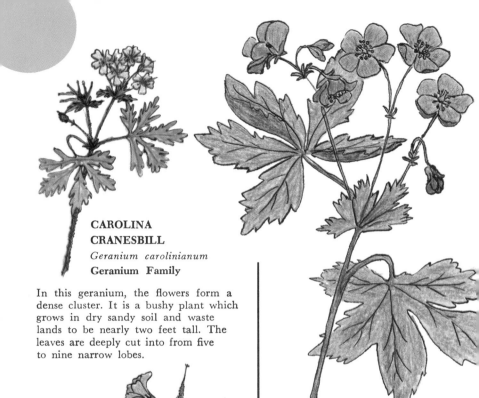

CAROLINA CRANESBILL
Geranium carolinianum
Geranium Family

In this geranium, the flowers form a dense cluster. It is a bushy plant which grows in dry sandy soil and waste lands to be nearly two feet tall. The leaves are deeply cut into from five to nine narrow lobes.

HERB-ROBERT
Geranium robertianum
Geranium Family

This flower grows in rocky woods, sha areas, and on shores to a height of nearly two feet. It has hairy, reddis stems, and fern-like leaves that are divided into three or five finely cut sections. The end segment of each ha its own stem. The flowers are one-ha inch broad, pink or reddish purple, and have unnotched petals. The lea have a disagreeable odor when crushe

98

WILD GERANIUM
OR SPOTTED CRANE'S BILL
Geranium maculatum
Geranium Family

The Wild Geranium has a lovely
lavender or purple-pink flower which
looks similar to a small wild rose or a
single apple blossom. The blossom is
about one inch in diameter and faces
upward.

The plant will reach a height of from
one to two feet. The gray-green leaves
are beautiful and deeply cut. They are
coarse and quite hairy or fuzzy. The
older leaves are sometimes spotted with
white or brown.

The lavender flowers have five rounded
petals which slightly fold over each
other at the base. The flowers are
arranged in small clusters at the end
of the branches. There are ten large
golden-brown anthers which can be
clearly seen. When the flower goes by,
the fruit bursts open and scatters seeds
for many feet in all directions.

The Wild Geranium blooms in the
fields, open woods and along shady
lanes from April to July. It may be
found all along the North Atlantic
coast and west to the Mississippi River.

MEADOW
CRANESBILL
Geranium pratense
Geranium Family

This variety of Geranium is similar to
Wild Geranium but has more
deeply cleft leaves with
seven narrow segments. The beak of
the fruit is densely hairy. The flowers
are a more blue-purple and the stalks
are wooly. It grows to a height of
from one to two feet and is more
prevalent in Northern New England
than the Wild Geranium is.

The leaves of this plant are fern-like
and not like those of the others on this
page. These leaves usually last through
the winter as a rosette on the ground.
The flowering stems rise from the
midst of these and at first are only a
few inches tall. The flowers are rose-
colored and are less than one-half of
an inch broad. Later the plant grows
taller and is more branching. Storks-
bill grows along roadsides in sandy
soil and is from three to twelve inches
tall. The flower's name comes from
the beaks on the plant. The beak,
when dried, separates from the central
column and becomes twisted like a
corkscrew.

STORKSBILL
or ALFILARIA
Erodium cicutarium
Geranium Family

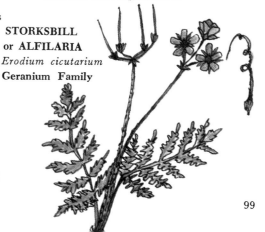

FIELD MILKWORT or POLYGALA
Polygala sanguinea
Milkwort Family

This polygala, though usually bright rose-purple, may also be greenish or even white. It grows in moist sunny meadows to a height of from two to twelve inches. The flower head is oblong and sometimes there are sever flower heads on one plant. The leave are alternately attached on the stem and the stem is sometimes branche All three of the Milkworts mention have concealed fertile fruit beneath tl ground surface.

RACEMED MILKWORT
Polygala polygama
Milkwort Family

This milkwort grows from four to twenty inches high in dry sandy soil or open sandy woods. The leaves are attached one at a time and the stem is very leafy. The showy rose-colored flowers are in a loose slender raceme at the top of the stalk. Each flower is about one-third inch long.

FRINGED POLYGALA or GAY WINGS
Polygala paucifol
Milkwort Family

Bird-On-The-Wing and Flowering Wintergreen are two other common names given to this little flower. It grows in sunny spots in the woods, at the bases of trees, and along stone walls. The plant is only about four inches tall, but has a root that is sometimes over a foot in length. The stem bends sharply as it enters the soil. Both leaves and flowers are clustered together at the top of the stem. The pink or magenta tube-like flower is made up of two pink sepals which are wing-shaped and three small petals which join together to form a hollow tube. Part of the third petal is fringed. The leaves and flower are both about an inch long, and the shiny leaves are sharply pointed.

This common creeping weed grows abundantly in farmyards, gardens, and in waste places. It has round or heart-shaped leaves that are from one to three inches broad. Each leaf is on its own leaf stem (petiole) and has from five to seven shallow lobes. The pink, lavender, or bluish-white blossoms are about one-half inch broad and have five heart-shaped petals. The flowers grow from the leaf axils. The stamens are united in a column around the pistil as in the Musk mallow. The fruit that forms after the flower fades resembles a flat round cheese. Perhaps this is why many people call this plant by another name — Cheeses.

COMMON MALLOW
Malva neglecta
Mallow Family

MUSK MALLOW
Malva moschata
Mallow Family

The Musk Mallow is a tall branching plant which grows in fields, along roadsides, and in waste places throughout the eastern states. The plant is often over two feet tall. The leaves are from one to four inches broad and are intricately cut into deep-toothed narrow segments. The flowers are one and one-half to two inches broad and have five notched petals. The flower gives off a light musk-scented odor. The flowers are usually clustered together at leafy ends of the stems or branches. The pink or white petals are several times larger than the green pointed triangular-shaped sepals beneath. The numerous stamens surround the pistil and form a column which rises from the center of the flower.

PURPLE LOOSESTRIFE
Lythrum salicaria
Loosestrife Family

This tall, beautiful weed grows in large colonies in swampy meadows, shores, and marshes and is a stunning mass of lavender or magenta when all of the flower spires are open. The stems are from two to five feet tall. The downy leaves are usually opposite each other on the stem, but are sometimes whorled in threes or fours. The flowers are one-half to two-thirds inch long and are in a dense terminal spike-like cluster. This spike also contains numerous small leaves that look like bracts. The blossom has either four or six petals and twice as many stamens as there are petals.

**HYSSOP-LEAVED
LOOSESTRIFE**
Lythrum hyssopifolia
Loosestrife Family

This loosestrife is smaller, from six to twenty-four inches tall, and is sometimes branched at the base. The pale green stem leaves are narrow and alternate. The flower is tiny, pale purple and is trumpet-shaped. (See enlarged flower). The six petals at the top are shorter than the tubular throat. At the base of the flower is a tiny leaf. Flowers are usually solitary, but are sometimes paired in the leaf axils.

**CLAMMY CUPHEA or
BLUE WAXWEED**
Cuphea petiolata
Loosestrife Family

Cuphea is from one to two feet tall and grows in dry soil of open woods and sandy fields. It has sticky, reddish hairs and paired leaves on long leaf stalks (petioles). The flowers are magenta or red-purple and are attached singly or in pairs in the axils of the upper leaves. The flowers have six uneven, clawed petals which protrude from the hairy, ribbed calyx which is about one-half of an inch long. This hairy calyx has an odd sac-like protuberance on the upper side so that — at quick glance — one might think the stem is attached to the side of the flower instead of at the end.

PURPLE-LEAVED WILLOW-HERB
Epilobium coloratum
Evening-Primrose Family

This hairy Willow-herb is erect and
freely branched. It grows in wet places
to a height of from one to three
feet. The leaves are narrow and lance-
shaped with numerous teeth.
Sometimes the leaves are marked with
purple. The numerous minute flowers
are less than one-fourth of an inch long
and have four white or pink petals.
The flowers are sometimes in a nodding
position. The numerous seed pods
are as long as two inches and stand
erect. They split open when mature to
expose the many seeds with white hairs.

NORTHERN WILLOW-HERB
Epilobium glandulosum
Evening-Primrose Family

This stout, leafy Willow-herb grows
in wet places to a height of from one
to three feet. It sends out stolons
similar to those on strawberry plants
to start new plants for the next year.
The toothed leaves are attached to the
stem without long petioles and the
leaves are not marked with purple.
The numerous pink flowers have four
petals and are erect. The seed pod
splits lengthwise to expose the seeds with
whitish hairs.

This fragrant wild flower grows in great patches on the floor of forests where there is an underlying sandy soil and a carpet of decaying leaves or pine needles. The plant grows to a height of from four to twelve inches. Numerous shiny green leaves are arranged in whorls or scattered along the stem. The leaves vary in size from one to two and one-half inches in length and are sharply toothed at the edges. The tips may be either blunt or pointed and the leaves remain bright green throughout the winter. The flowers are arranged in a loose cluster at the top of the leaf-bearing stalk. The flowers are about one-half inch broad and vary in color from white to dark pink. The five petals are noticeably cup-shaped, rounded at the tips, and widely spread. Ten deep violet anthers are evenly arranged like beads around the flat-topped central pistil.

The common name, Pipsissewa, is probably of Indian origin. Some authorities on Indian culture state that the red men felt that this evergreen plant possessed great strength-giving properties.

PIPSISSEWA or PRINCE'S PINE
Chimaphila umbellata var. cisatlantica
Heath Family

SPOTTED WINTERGREEN
Chimaphila maculata
Heath Family

This woodland plant is also called Spotted Pipsissewa, and indeed it is very similar to Pipsissewa on page 104. It grows from an underground stem and has erect branches with leaves that remain green all winter. It is from four to ten inches tall. The nodding waxy flowers are fragrant and can be either white or pink. They have five recurved petals and ten stamens which form a crown in the center. The round tip of the pistil (stigma) forms the central point of the crown. The long leaves are arranged in whorls of four. They are toothed, sharply pointed, and have a whitish pattern at the midvein.

ONE-FLOWERED WINTERGREEN
Moneses uniflora
Heath Family

This tiny flower is seldom taller than five inches. It grows in mossy, sheltered woods. The leaves are tiny, round, and finely toothed. A solitary pink or white flower hangs face down from the tip of the stem. It is fragrant and very similar to the flower described above.

PINK PYROLA
Pyrola asarifolia
Heath Family

This pyrola has shining, round, leaf-blades which are indented or heart-shaped at the base. The leaves form a rosette at the base of the single flower stem. Flowers form a slender spike-like cluster and are similar to those of other Pyrolas described on page 56 in the white section, but these petals vary from crimson to pale pink.

TRAILING ARBUTUS
Epigaea repens
Heath Family

The common name for this tiny
fragrant spring flower is *Mayflower*.
One may find patches of rusty evergreen
leaves during the late winter and very
early spring. These have hidden and
protected buds which were formed
the previous fall and winter. One must
lift the leaves to find the tiny exquisite
white or pale pink flowers.
The plant is a creeping evergreen with
a woody stem. The leaves are oval
shaped with rounded ends. Often the
leaves are spotted with brown or areas
of decay. The plant usually grows to
be four or five inches high.
A few flowers are clustered together
at the end of the woody stems that
trail over the ground. Each flower
has five petals which are joined

together at the base to form a tubula
flower. Though these fragrant flowers
appear before the last of the snow i
gone, the new leaves do not unfold un
June.
Thoughtless people have pulled this
flower up by the roots and it has
become very rare where once it wa
plentiful. Some states are considerin
passing a law to prohibit the
picking of this plant without consent
the land owner. Enjoy these flowers
but do not destroy them for future
generations.

BOG LAUREL
Kalmia polifolia
Heath Family

Bog Laurel is a smaller shrub found in bogs — usually less than three feet tall. It is sparingly branched and has leaves which are arranged in pairs. The edges of the leaves are rolled backwards and the under sides of the leaves are covered with white hairs. The flowers are similar to the Mountain Laurel but are smaller and paler in color.

MOUNTAIN LAUREL
Kalmia latifolia
Heath Family

Mountain Laurel is an evergreen shrub usually about three feet tall. Where it is abundant, however, it grows to be as tall as ten feet and forms dense thickets. The leaves are alternate on the woody stem and are shiny and leathery. The cluster of blossoms is made up of cup-shaped pink flowers with five petals joined together. There are ten stamens which form arching spokes from the center of the flower to tiny pits on the side of the flower. These are released when insects light on the flowers.

SHEEP LAUREL or LAMBKILL
Kalmia angustifolia
Heath Family

This branching shrub grows up to 3 ft. tall but is usually about fifteen or twenty inches tall. It grows in pastures, rocky slopes, and in swamps. The cuplike flowers form in a cluster at the end of last year's growth of leaves, and the new leaves seem to grow upwards from the middle of this cluster of flowers. The leaves occur in 3's along the stem. The older leaves below are narrow and are in a drooping position. Sometimes the underside of the leaf is hairy.

**EARLY AZALEA or
MOUNTAIN AZALEA**
Rhododendron roseum
Heath Family

This is a much-branched shrub —
often over six feet tall — which
grows in moist or dry woods,
especially at higher elevations.
The leaves have soft, white, wooly
hair on the underside. The twigs
and buds are also wooly.
Very fragrant bright pink flowers,
which sometimes appear before the
leaves, are shaped like a flaring tube.
The tube is about the same length
as the petals, but the stamens and
pistil protrude from it. The five
petals usually fold backwards.

RHODORA
*Rhododendron
canadense*
Heath Family

Rhodora is a branching shrub up
to three feet tall which grows in
bogs and on rocky slopes or wet woods.
The magenta flowers open before
the leaves. The flowers have a
three-lobed upper lip and two narrow
spreading lobes below. Curving pink
or purple stamens protrude from
the center of the flower.
The flower does not have a long
trumpet as do most members of this
genus. The leaves, which develop
after the flowers fade, are narrow
and oblong and are finely hairy
on the underside.

**PINKSTER-FLOWER or
PINK AZALEA**
*Rhododendron
nudiflorum*
**Heath
Family**

This azalea is very similar to the
Early Azalea at the top of the page,
the protruding stamens and pistil are
longer and more curved. The flower
odorless and the tube is much longer.
The color of the flower varies from
pink to nearly white. The buds
are often nearly red — thus giving
a lovely two-toned effect. The bud
twigs, and leaves of this plant are
not as hairy as the Early Azalea.

108

This small spreading cranberry grows in bogs and on wet or dry mossy, rocky slopes to a height of from two to seven inches. The stem is quite woody and has small, oval, glossy-green leaves with tiny black dots on the underside of the leaf. There are only a few pink and white variegated flowers in a small, tight, terminal cluster. Each flower has four petals which are joined together about half way from the base. Each petal is puffed outward — not restricted or curved backwards as in other Heath Family plants. The fruit is a berry maturing in late summer and makes a delicious sauce.

MOUNTAIN CRANBERRY or COWBERRY
Vaccinium vitis-idaea
Heath Family

LARGE CRANBERRY
Vaccinium macrocarpon
Heath Family

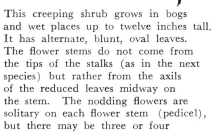

This creeping shrub grows in bogs and wet places up to twelve inches tall. It has alternate, blunt, oval leaves. The flower stems do not come from the tips of the stalks (as in the next species) but rather from the axils of the reduced leaves midway on the stem. The nodding flowers are solitary on each flower stem (pedicel), but there may be three or four

pedicels on each plant. Flowers are pink and have four petals that turn back so far they often overlap at the top. The red and yellow stamens protrude from the center to form a "beak". The fruit is a juicy, seedy berry which matures in late fall and is used in making cranberry sauce.

SMALL CRANBERRY
Vaccinium oxycoccus
Heath Family

This cranberry is very similar to the one above, but the leaves are smaller and the flowers are on pedicels which grow only at the ends of the leafy stalks. There are two tiny reddish bracts about mid-way on the flower pedicel. The flowers are about the same as large cranberry. The leaves are more pointed and the edges roll under. The underside of the leaf is whitish.

SEA MILKWORT
Glaux maritima
Primrose Family

Sea Milkwort is a pale fleshy plant which often rests on the ground. It grows on beaches and at the edges of salt marshes to a height of from two to six inches. It is a branching plant with narrow, oblong, or linear leaves which end in a blunt point. A tiny flower with five petal-like sepals is tucked into the axil of each leaf. The flower usually is pink, but may vary from white to crimson.

This dwarf primrose grows on wet banks, gravelly shores, or on rocks t height of from six to twelve inches The leaves are arranged in a ring at bottom of the flower stalk. The base of the leaf is tapering and the marg are toothed. The leaves are smooth, but the lower sides are often cov with a white or yellow powder. The flowers are funnel-shaped and may either pink or pale purple. Usually there is a yellow eye. The flowers are in a loose cluster of from two to eig at the top of the single flower stalk. Each flower has a five-lobed corolla and is from one-half to three-fourth of an inch broad.

BIRD'S-EYE PRIMROSE
Primula mistassinica
Primrose Family

Scarlet Pimpernel is an erect, branching plant which grows on lawns, in gardens, and along roadsides to a height of four to twelve inches. The paired, oval leaves are pointed and have no leaf stem. They are attached directly to the main stem. The star-like scarlet flowers have five petals and only open in fair weather. Each flower is on its own slender pedicel which rises from the axil of the leaf.

SCARLET PIMPERNEL
Anagallis arvensis
Primrose Family

CROWBERRY
Empetrum nigrum
Heath Family

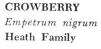

This much-branching, woody-stemmed plant forms a thick spreading mat over rocks and bare ground. It is an arctic plant which grows at higher elevations and along ocean shores to a height of less than six inches. Numerous needle-like leaves are crowded on the stems. The leaves are less than one-fourth inch long. The minute flowers have three sepals and three petals and are pinkish, greenish, or purplish. They are tucked in the axils of the tiny leaves. The fruit is black and berry-like and ripens in July. It is inedible.

This interesting and beautiful plant can be found in late April and early May in open woods, on prairies, and on moist cliffs. The gray-green leaves are oblong and are found at the base of the flower stalk which grows from eight to twenty-four inches tall. The flowers are gathered together in a showy cluster at the end of the flower stalk. Each shooting star has its own curved support which branches from the main stalk. The crown of petals (corolla) is reversed and appears to be put on backwards. There are five petals which may be purple, rose, or white. The stamens protrude from the throat of the flower and the golden anthers form a cone which protects the female part (pistil) of the flower. The base of the petals are often spotted with dark purple.

SHOOTING STAR or AMERICAN COWSLIP
Dodecatheon meadia
Primrose Family

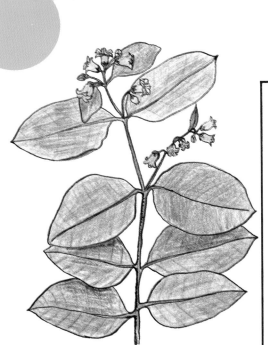

SPREADING DOGBANE or INDIAN HEMP
Apocynum androsaemifolium
Dogbane Family

Spreading Dogbane is a shrubby plant
with ruddy-colored stems that are
so branching there is no evidence
of one main stem. The stems are
not woody and will bend easily.
A milky juice comes from the stem
if it is broken. Along the ruddy
stem are pairs of large, oval leaves.
This plant grows in thickets and
along paths and roadsides to a
height of from one to three feet.
Numerous flowers are in loose
clusters at the ends of the branches.
Each fragrant, bell-shaped flower
hangs on its own curved stem.
They are pale pink and are striped
inside with deep rose. The five
teeth on the bell curve outwards.

PURPLE MILKWEED
Asclepias purpurascens
Milkweed Family

Purple Milkweed grows in woods a
thickets to a height of two to three
feet. It is smaller, but very similar to
Common Milkweed, but has deep
magenta-red flowers with dark purp
petals. The leaves are more pointed
and the hood-like cups are taller an
hide the horns completely. The po
are wooly, but not warty as those o
the Common Milkweed.

Instead of illustrating the entire pla
a single flower has been drawn to
show a typical milkweed blossom com
to all on this page — with minor
variations, of course. The enlarged
petal below shows the slender horn
or hood which is on the inside of
milkweed petals.

BLUNT-LEAVE MILKWEE
*Asclepi
amplexicau*
Milkweed Family

COMMON MILKWEED
Asclepias syriaca
Milkweed Family

This stout, downy plant grows along roads and in dry fields to a height of from three to six feet. The broad oval leaves are thick and are covered with a grayish down on the underside. The flowers are in numerous round umbels at the top of the plant and in upper leaf axils. The umbels are sometimes so heavy that they are in a drooping position. The flowers are in soft shades of rose, lavender, pink, and dull, brownish purple. The erect pointed seed pods are gray-green and have a warty appearance. The pods are up to four inches long.

FOUR-LEAVED MILKWEED
Asclepias quadrifolia
Milkweed Family

This milkweed has whorls of four pointed, oval leaves, but at the top of the plant the leaves may only be in pairs. The leaves have long stalks (petioles). The plant grows in dry woods to a height of from one to two and one-half feet. There are several loose clusters of flowers at the top, and the flowers are pale pink or lavender and often have whitish hoods.

This milkweed is a small plant which grows in dry soil to a height of from two to three feet. It can be identified by its wavy-edged leaves which clasp the stem at the base. The flowers are greenish-purple with pink hoods. Usually there is only one flower umbel on each plant. The seed pods are more slender than those of the Common Milkweed, and they are practically smooth.

This member of the morning-glory family grows in a trailing or twining manner and is often several feet long. It grows in fields, on beaches, in thickets, along roadsides, and climbs over fences, stonewalls, hedgerows, and old compost heaps.

The leaves are arrowhead-shaped with blunt basal lobes which point away from the center vein.

The leaves vary in size from two to five inches long. Each leaf has its own leaf stem which is attached to the main twining stem.

The flowers are shaped like a funnel and are usually pink with white stripes. They vary from pale pink to white, however, and often fade with age. There are five lobes on the spreading mouth of the trumpet-shaped flower. The five stamens are attached at the base of the tube, but the tips or anthers often protrude from center.

HEDGE BINDWEED

Convolvulus sepium

Morning-Glory Family

WIL
SWEET WILLIA
Phlox macula
Phlox Fam

114

MOSS PINK or GROUND PHLOX
Phlox sublata
Phlox Family

Moss Pink is a low creeping plant that spreads over rocky or sandy land. It carpets hillsides and is commonly found in cemeteries or along lanes. The stem of this plant is much branched, and crowded with stiff-pointed leaves, but only grows a few inches high. The ends of the branches turn upwards and end in clusters of five-petaled tube-like flowers. The flowers bloom simultaneously and hide the moss-type foliage from view.

This mass of flowers can be breathtakingly beautiful when viewed from a distance. The colors range from white to bright pink, to orchid, but pink is the most common.

This is similar to the above plant, but the flowers are fragrant and usually are more bluish-pink. The flowers are arranged in a flat-topped cluster at the top of the stem. Each flower is about an inch long and often the five petals are deeply notched at the ends. Blue Phlox grows in moist woods and thickets to a height of from nine to eighteen inches. There are oblong basal leaves and stem leaves that are opposite each other on the stem.

his wild flower is similar to the garden ariety, but has a slender purple-potted stem and the flowers are arranged a long cylindrical cluster. The wers have five pink petals which e joined to make a long corolla tube. here are five pointed green sepals at e base of the long tube. This plant from one and one-half to three et tall and grows in low woods and ear river banks. It has opposite notched leaves which are smooth d firm.

WILD BLUE PHLOX
Phlox divaricata
Phlox Family

HOUND'S TONGUE
Cynoglossum officinale
Forget-Me-Not Family

This downy plant has a "mousy odor."
It grows in fields, waste places, and
along roadsides to a height of from
two to three feet. The flowers have
five petals and are dull
reddish-purple and about one-third
of an inch across. The hairy,
four-part fruit has hooked bristles
which cause it to stick to animals
and clothing of people as they pass by.
The lower leaves have stalks, but
the upper ones are attached directly
on the main stem.

COMFREY
Symphytum officinale
Forget-Me-Not Family

This erect, hairy plant has branching
stems and is from two to three feet tall.
It grows along roadsides and in
waste places. The leaves do not
have a petiole (leaf stem), but
rather extend downward on the main
stem to form long wings on either
side. The leaves have very
noticeable veins which stand out
on the under side. They are lighter
in color than the leaf, and form an
odd pattern on the leaf.
The tubular flowers are in curled
clusters which are characteristic
of flowers in the Forget-Me-Not
family. The flowers may be white,
cream, pale pink, or dull purple and
are about one-third of an inch across.

HOARY VERVAIN
Verbena stricta
Vervain Family

Hoary Vervain grows in fields, rocky
open places, or along roadsides to
a height of from one to four feet.
The tall stem may be simple, but is
usually branching. The leaves are
thick, coarsely toothed, and have
very short stalks (or none at all)
where the base of the leaf is attached
to the main stem. The stems and
leaves are densely covered with
fine white hairs. The flowers are
arranged in long, thick, compact
spikes, and only part of the spike is
opened at one time. Each flower
is funnel-shaped with either a
straight or a curved tube.
It has two lips with five lobes.
The color is a pale purple or a
rosy-pink. This is one way to tell it
from Blue Vervain which is similar,
but has deep blue flowers.

NARROW-LEAVED VERVAIN
Verbena simplex
Vervain Family

This smaller vervain is from four to
twenty inches tall and is usually
sparingly branched. It has slender
spikes of lavender or light purple
flowers. It is easily identified from
other vervains by its long, lanceolate
leaves which taper to a stalkless base.

Red Dead Nettle resembles Henbit
in habit and size. The square
stem has long spaces without any
leaves and there is a short, leafy
cluster at the top. The flowers
are tucked among the leaves.
The reddish or purplish flowers have
a ring of hairs near the base.
The upper lip is about a third as
long as the tube.

HENBIT
Lamium
amplexicaule
Mint Family

Henbit has several branching, square
stems which spring from one root.
It is from four to sixteen inches tall
and grows in wastelands and
along roadsides.
There are a few long-stemmed basil
leaves with scalloped edges.
The wide, stem leaves are roundish
with scalloped edges, and
surround the stem in pairs.
The flowers are clustered in the
axils of the upper leaves.
The tubed flower (see enlargement)
is opened wide at the top and the
upper lip forms a hood over
the lower, lobed lip.
The flower varies from white to
pinkish purple and has darker spots
on it. The upper lip is crowned
with a tuft of magenta hairs.

BASIL
Satureja vulgaris
Mint Family

Basil has square, creeping stems from
which hairy, flowering branches rise
from one to two feet. The paired
leaves are hairy and slightly toothed.
The numerous, tubular, lipped flowers
are pale purple or pink. They are in
dense heads at the tips of the branches
with a pair of leaves below each head.
The cluster looks wooly for there are
white hairs on the calyx and bracts.

118

HEMP-NETTLE
Galeopsis tetrahit
Mint Family

Hemp-Nettle has either simple or
branched, hairy, square stems with
an enlarged place below each pair
of leaves. The leaves are lance-
shaped, toothed, and have hairs on
both sides. The flowers are small
but are massed together at the
leaf axils. The tubular flower
(see enlargement) is white, or pink,
or variegated — with stiff, white
hairs on the top of the upper lip.
The flower is strongly two-lipped
with the upper lip forming a hood
over the three-lobed lower lip.
The calyx at the base of the tubular
flower has five sharp spines on it.

CURLED MINT
*Mentha aquatica
var. crispa*
Mint Family

This mint blooms earlier than other
wild mints. It grows in wet spots
and in ditches to a height of from
one and a half to three feet.
The broad leaves are attached directly
to the square stem in pairs.
The margins of the leaves are crisp
and have very ragged teeth.
The numerous tiny flowers are in a
tight cylindrical or round cluster
at the summit of the stem.
This plant has probably escaped
from cultivation, for it is often
planted as an ornamental.

PAINTED CUP or INDIAN PAINT-BRUSH
Castilleja coccinea
Snapdragon Family

Painted Cup is a hairy plant which
grows in fields and meadows or in
damp sandy soil. It grows to a
height of from one to two feet.
The leaves vary greatly, but all have
several long narrow parts — with the
middle segment being the longest.
The leaf bracts at the top of the
stem have three lobes and are tipped
with scarlet. These nearly hide the
small two-lipped greenish-yellow
flowers, but the pistils protrude
from among the scarlet-tipped leaves.

This hairy weed is common in fields
and waste places. It grows to a height
of from four to sixteen inches.
It can be either branched or not
branched. The leaves are narrow
and have two or three blunt teeth
on each leaf margin. The flowers
are in a leafy spike at the top.
Pairs of leaves are mixed right in
with the pink flowers.
Each flower is about a half-inch long
and has two lips. The bottom lip
has three lobes and the top lip is
hood-like and does not fold backwards.
The top lip is often covered with
light red hairs.

WOOD BETONY or LOUSEWORT
Pedicularis canadensis
Snapdragon Family

RED BARTSIA
Odontites serotina
Snapdragon Family

is hairy plant grows in woods and
arings to a height of from
r to twelve inches. It has tubular
oded flowers in a cluster at the
s of the stems. The upper lip has
o slender teeth below the rounded
nmit. The lower lip is lighter
color and shorter than the top lip.
e bunch of blossoms at the top
pears to rest on a cushion of
dish-green deeply cut leaves.
e color of the flower varies, but
usually tones of bronze, red, or
rple with a yellowish lower lip.
e leaves are long and slender but
very deeply cut. Often as the
around it becomes dry, the leaves
the plant turn to bronze or
dish-green.

HAIRY BEARDTONGUE
Penstemon hirsutus
Snapdragon Family

There are over fifteen species of
this plant in our area but all have
one common characteristic — a tufted
stamen which nearly fills the throat
of the tubular flower. This species
grows in rocky woods and dry fields
to a height of from one to three feet.
The stems stand erect — usually
several coming from the same
rootstalk. In most species, the tops
of the leaves and the stem are hairy.
The leaves are long, slender, pointed,
and have toothed margins.
The pale lavender petals are fused
into a slender tube about an inch long.
The inside of the tube is covered
with pale hairs. The upper lip is
two-lobed and erect, but the lower lip
points straight out.

BLUE TOAD FLAX
Linaria canadensis
Snapdragon Family

This erect plant is from four to
thirty inches tall and grows in dry
sandy soil. The shiny leaves are very
narrow and are scattered along the
stem. The small bluish flowers are
tubular and arranged in long
racemes. The entire flower is
about one-third inch long and has a
slender spur at the base.
The lips are much longer than the
tube and the bottom lip has two
short white ridges on it.
Around the base of the plant is a
circle of runners with tiny leaves.

VIRGINIA WATERLEAF or JOHN'S CABBAGE
Hydrophyllum virginianum
Waterleaf Family

This hairy plant grows in rich woods
and along streams to a height of
from one to three feet. The flowers
are white or pale violet and are in
coiled clusters which unroll as they
bloom. The stamens protrude far
beyond the petals, giving a "fuzzy"
appearance to the cluster.
The barrel-shaped flower is made up
of five petals which do not flare
outward. The calyx is pointed and
is bristly. The flower clusters are
on long stalks high above the leaves.
The leaves, which often appear
stained or water spotted, have from
five to seven lobes with jagged teeth.
The stem is reddish at the joints.

WATER-WILLOW
Justica americana
Acanthus Family

This plant grows in shallow water
or on wet shores to a height of
from one to three feet. It has
slender willow-like leaves in pairs.
The flowers are in small, long-stem
clusters which rise from axils of leav
Each flower is bicolored — the
upper hood-like lip is pale violet
or reddish violet and the lower
three-lobed lip is white with
reddish spots or marks.

This delicate plant of the cold wo
bogs, and peaty places has a creepi
stem from which short erect bran
rise. Nodding trumpet-shaped flow
hang in pairs from the tip of the
branched stem. Each flower is ab
one-half inch long and has five
small teeth. It is very fragrant. T
stalk is very slender and from thre
to six inches tall. The leaves are
very small and round and are
arranged in pairs.

This low creeping plant grows in rich woods. The pink or white four-petaled flowers are joined together in pairs at the end of the trailing branches. The petals are hairy on the inside. The shiny evergreen leaves are small and nearly round with lighter colored veins. They are arranged in pairs along the stem. The fruit is a single red berry which develops from the bottom parts of both flowers. The berry has two blossom ends instead of only one as do most other berries.

PARTRIDGE-BERRY or RUNNING BOX
Mitchella repens
Bedstraw Family

This smooth, high-climbing vine is found in thickets and open woods along streams and low ground. There are whorls of slender trumpet-shaped flowers from one and one-half to two inches long. The outside is bright red, but the inside is yellow. The upper leaves are roundish and their bases join together around the stem. The lower leaves are somewhat more pointed and are often hairy on the underside.

TRUMPET HONEYSUCKLE
Lonicera sempervirens
Honeysuckle Family

TWINFLOWER
Linnaea borealis
Honeysuckle Family

This plant has wiry, much-branched
stems with leaves that are very deeply
cut into very narrow, grass-like leaflets.
Spotted Knapweed grows in fields,
waste places, and along roads to a
height of from one to four feet.
The flowers are pink, purple, or white
and are arranged in numerous heads
at the ends of the many branches.
Each head is in a thimble-shaped
receptacle which is covered with
overlapping, black-fringed bracts.

**SPOTTED
KNAPWEED**
Centaurea maculosa
Composite Family

BUTTERBUR or BUTTERFLY DOCK

Petasites hybridus
Composite Family

Butterbur has huge, roundish, basal
leaves which are sometimes two feet
across.   The stout stems are hollow
and from four to sixteen inches tall
when in flower.   After the flower
goes to seed, however, the plant may
grow to be as tall as forty inches.
There are numerous flower heads
in a long club-like cluster.
The flowers are tiny, lilac-pink or
purple with white anthers.
There are no ray flowers present as
there are in most members of the
Composite Family.

TYROL KNAPWEED
Centaurea dubia
Composite Family

Tyrol Knapweed is similar to Spotted Knapweed, but the leaves are not deeply lobed and the flower heads are smaller. The lower leaves have long petioles (leaf stems) and are spoon-shaped in general outline, but are unevenly lobed. The upper stem leaves are smaller and have no petioles. These are not lobed, but merely toothed. The heads are at the ends of the numerous branches. The marginal flowers on the flower head are greatly enlarged, and at close observation one can see five petal-like lobes on each ray flower. The light-colored bracts have conspicuous black marks at the tips. The plant as a whole is from eight to forty inches tall and grows in fields and along roads.

All Fleabanes have very numerous thread-like ray flowers in the flower heads. This species has as many as one hundred and fifty. Common Fleabane is a slender, hairy plant with few to many deep pink, pale magenta, or white flower heads which are less than an inch across. The basal leaves are narrow, lobed, and spoon-shaped in general outline. The stem leaves are smaller and embrace the stem. The plant is from six to twenty-eight inches tall and grows in just about every type of environment.

**COMMON
FLEABANE**
*Erigeron
philadelphicus*
Composite Family

PASTURE THISTLE
Cirsium pumilum
Composite Family

This thistle has the largest flowering head of any species in our area. It grows in dry soil in pastures, old fields, or open woods to a height of about one to three feet. The stems are very hairy, but are *not winged* as the stems in the next thistle. The lobed leaves are pale on the underside and have long spines. There are only a few flower heads on each plant, and many times there is only a solitary head from two to three inches across. The head is sweet-scented and purple-pink to white.

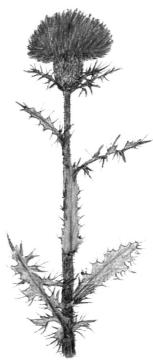

BULL THISTLE
Cirsium vulgare
Composite Family

This large thistle grows from two to six feet high along roadsides, in fields, and in waste places. It can be distinguished from the Pasture Thistle by the conspicuous *spiny wings* on the stems and the rigid, yellow-tipped spines on the flower bracts. The heads are reddish-purple and the stems are sometimes reddish or just tinged with red at the leaf axils. The spiny leaves are pale and wooly on the underside.

Other names for this lily are Field
Lily or Wild Yellow Lily. It is more
typically a yellow lily, but the color
varies from yellow to orange to almost
red. The plant is from two to five
feet tall and grows in moist open
places or wet meadows. Canada Lily
has clusters of up to twenty bell-
shaped flowers — each on its own
pedicel (flower stem). The flowers
are in a nodding position at the
summit of the stem or from the axils
of upper leaves. There are six petals
which curve outwards, but not
backwards. There are large dark
spots on the inside of the petals. The
long, pointed leaves are usually in
whorls at intervals around the slender
stem.

CANADA LILY
Lilium canadense
Lily Family

WOOD LILY
Lilium philadelphicum
Lily Family

DAY LILY
Hemerocallis fulva
Lily Family

This lily grows from a bulb on an
erect stem from one to three feet tall
in dry woods or thickets. There are
from one to five flowers at the
summit which face upward. The
leaves are in whorls around the stem.
The six petals are usually a brilliant
orange, but vary from yellow-orange
to nearly red. There are purple
spots on the inside of the petals near
the base.

This tawny-orange lily faces upward
also, but may be distinguished from
the Wood Lily because it has *no
spots* and has a *leafless stem*. The
long sword-like leaves grow in a
clump at the base of the plant. There
are clusters of long buds at the top
of the stem, and each opens for
one day only and then fades as
another bud opens. Five long
stamens and the pistil protrude from
the throat of the funnel-shaped flower.
The plant is from three to six feet
tall and is not a native wild flower,
but has escaped from cultivation.

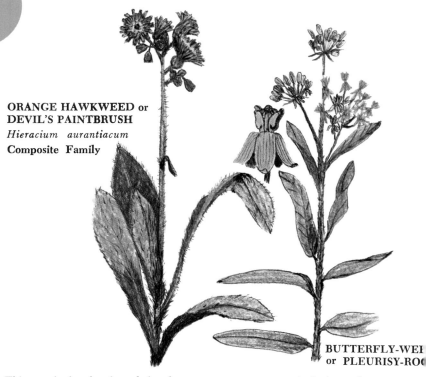

ORANGE HAWKWEED or DEVIL'S PAINTBRUSH
Hieracium aurantiacum
Composite Family

BUTTERFLY-WEE[or PLEURISY-ROO[

Asclepias tuberosa
Milkweed Family

This particular hawkweed is always bright red-orange. It is a very hairy plant with long, tapering, basal leaves. Sometimes there are one or two reduced leaves on the stem, but not usually. Orange Hawkweed grows to a height of from six to twenty-four inches along roads and paths, and often covers an entire field. The flower heads are in tight terminal clusters at the summit of the stem. Some flower heads open soon while others are still closed in round or oval black, hairy buds. Each head opens to from one-half to one inch broad. What appear to be orange strap-shaped petals with five teeth at the ends are not petals at all. These are really complete individual ray flowers.

This milkweed can easily be distinguished from other milkweeds by the bright orange flowers. The stout, hairy stems are from one t two feet high and are not milky wh broken. The long, narrow, pointed leaves are hairy and alternate on the stem — possibly opposite on smaller branches. The bright orang flowers are numerous and are in a terminal cluster. Look at the inset t see a typical milkweed-like blossom. The hoods on the flowers are erect and longer than the stamens. Insid of each hood is an odd-looking horn. The five petals drop down around the stem.

128

BLACKBERRY LILY
Belamcanda chinensis
Iris Family

This is not a lily, but an iris. It grows to a height of from one to two feet in open woods, along roadsides, and in dry places. It has escaped from cultivation and now grows wild in some places. The flower has six equal salmon-orange petals with crimson markings and is about two inches broad. The buds open one at a time and each flower lasts for only one day. The narrow leaves are similar to those of most iris plants.

The name Blackberry Lily was probably given to this plant because of the fruit. The oblong seed pod splits open when it is dry to reveal a blackberry-like cluster of shiny black seeds.

The Hoary Puccoon is found in open woods, on plains, and in dry sandy soil. It is from six to twenty inches tall and has curled-over clusters of yellow or orange flowers. Each individual flower has five flat lobes which form into a tube that hides the stamens. The small flower is about one-half of an inch long and in terminal leafy racemes. The leaves are very slender and are alternate on the stem. The stem and leaves are covered with stiff hairs.

**HOARY
PUCCOON**
Lithospermum canescens
Forget-Me-Not Family

129

SWEET FLAG
Acorus calamus
Arum Family

Sweet Flag is a tall grass-like plant
which grows in wet swampy places. It
has long stiff, sword-like leaves which
are as tall as four feet. There is a spadix
of closely crowded tiny greenish-yellow
flowers which jut out from the main
stem at an angle. The stem is flat
and very similar to the blade of leaf.
The rootstock of the Sweet Flag is very
spicy-smelling and furnishes materials
to make a drug called calamus.

GOLDEN CLUB
Orontium aquaticum
Arum Family

Golden Club is also a water-loving
member of the Arum Family. It grows i
swamps, ponds, and streams and ofter
stands in water so deep that the long
stalked leaves must float on the surfae
of the water. The oblong blue-green
leaves are water resistent. The plant
itself is often from one to two feet hig
The bright yellow flowers, though
very tiny, have from four to six golde
sepals and both male and female parts
They are crowded together and give
the appearance of a single mass — inst
of separate individual flowers. They
are on the spadix which is a club-
shaped structure at the end of the
flower stalk. The stalk usually has
curve in it and the club-like mass o
yellow flowers tilts to one side.

YELLOW STAR-GRASS
Hypoxis hirsuta
Amaryllis Family

Yellow Star-Grass is a common spring flower which grows in the open woods and meadows. It has a long blooming season and is particularly attractive when growing together with Blue-Eyed Grass.
The flower has a clear yellow inside and a green hairy outside. The leaves are hairy and grass-like. Each plant has several pointed star-like flowers on separate flowering stalks which are usually shorter than the leaves. The entire plant grows from a corm to a height of from three to seven inches.

These two Grass-like plants, are in two different families. There are about twelve species of the Yellow-Eyed Grass and all are similar to the one pictured. They are classified according to small technicalities, so it would be wise for the beginner to just learn the one name for all.
Yellow-Eyed Grass is a tufted grass-like plant which grows in wet meadows, bogs, or at the shore. The flower-bearing stalks are taller than the leaves. This stalk varies with the species, but may be as high as two or three feet in some cases. The flowers, held in a "cup" of overlapping scales, are bright yellow and have three petals. Three stamens and a three-branched style protrude from the center.

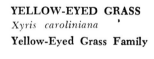

YELLOW-EYED GRASS
Xyris caroliniana
Yellow-Eyed Grass Family

YELLOW CLINTONIA or
BLUE BEAD LILY
Clintonia borealis
Lily Family

This lovely lily-like plant grows in the cool, moist woods and likes the shade. It is a member of the lily family so has the same type of vein-marked leaves. These large wide leaves are actually more striking than the small blossom. Each plant has from two to four shiny green leaves. From amidst these leaves, a single flower stalk rises. At the tip of the stalk, from three to six yellow bell-shaped flowers will hang. These are cream-colored or light yellow and look like miniature lilies.

Though the blossom itself is not too attractive, the berries which form later make up for this. The cluster of pure blue berries above the shiny wide leaves makes a distinctive picture. Blue is a rare color among wild flowers, but this uncommon color is striking on this Clintonia. For this reason, many call it the *Blue Bead Lily*.

The plant grows to be about a foot high, but varies more or less depending upon the habitat.

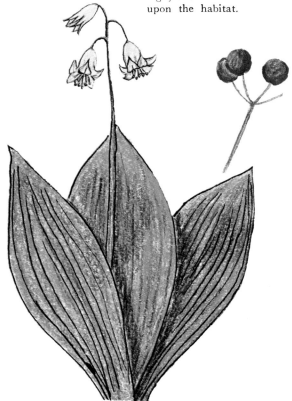

DOGTOOTH VIOLET
Erythronium americanum
Lily Family

This early spring flower can be found at the edge of moist woods and in thickets all along the eastern part of Canada and the United States. Dogtooth Violets grow in patches and each plant is from six to ten inches high.

The Dogtooth Violet has two long, flat, slender leaves which usually point in opposite directions. These leaves are a pale gray-green color and are speckled with white or purple.

Each plant has a flower stalk which rises from the ground and bears a single nodding lily-like flower. Each flower has six yellow petal-like parts which curl backwards when the plant is in full bloom. The outside of the flower is a pale or brownish yellow but the inside of the petals are bright yellow with rich brown spots. Six golden-brown stamens can be easily seen hanging below the up-turned petals.

This plant has many common names — most of which do not seem to fit the plant. Dogtooth Violet is a misleading name, for this flower is a member of the lily family and is not a violet. Adder's Tongue and Fawn Lily are two other names. Perhaps the mottled leaves suggested the spotted coat of an adder or a fawn and thus these names were given to this plant. Trout Lily is perhaps the most fitting common name, because the plant is a lily and is often found blooming along brooks about the time when trout season opens.

SOLOMON'S SEAL
Polygonatum pubescens
Lily Family

There are several species of this plant, but all have the same general leaf and plant structure. The stem grows in an arching fashion from the root; the leaves get smaller as they near the tip of the stem; and the veins are lengthwise on the leaves. The small greenish-white or yellow-white flowers are tubular and hang in pairs where the leaves join on to the stalk. The name Solomon's Seal comes from the scars on the rootstock. The leafy stem dies each winter and gets a new stem the following spring. Each time a stem dies, it leaves a scar similar to the seal of Solomon on the root. One can tell how old the plant is by counting the scars on the root. Solomon's Seal grows in woods in shady areas. The young shoots may be eaten, as may the berries.

But, unless you are absolutely sure what they are, it is unwise to eat any berries, for many are poisonous. See pages 173 for other species of Solomon's Seals.

This small early flower has many common names. Oakesia, Little Bellflow Sessile-Leaved Bellwort and Sessile Merrybells are only a few. The flow is very plentiful in Northern New England and thrives in woods or thickets. It is from six to twelve inch high and rises from a very short root. Each plant has a single straw-colored flower shaped like a long bell which hangs down from the end of a drooping branch. Each bellflower has six petal-like parts. There is an odor, but the drooping position of the flower hides it. The leaves are long and pointed and are attached right on the stem itself.

The flower in the center below is the Large-Flowered Bellwort. It has a smooth, leafy, forked stem. The leaves clasp the stem and sometimes are not completely opened when the flower blooms. The leaves are slightly hairy on the underside and are from two to five inches long — but smaller at the tip of the plant. The flower is drooping and bellshaped, and is a brighter yellow than the merrybells. The flower is sometimes over an inch long on a healthy plant.

This bellwort is from five to sixteen inches high and grows in moist woods. It has a single pale yellow flower. The stems seem to pierce the leaves. The inside of the flower is rough and has orange grains and is smaller than the flower on the Large-Flowered Bellwort.

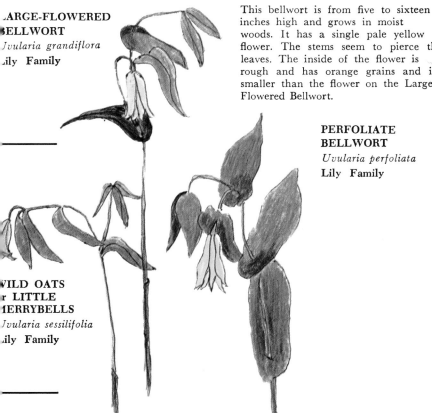

LARGE-FLOWERED BELLWORT
Uvularia grandiflora
Lily Family

PERFOLIATE BELLWORT
Uvularia perfoliata
Lily Family

WILD OATS or LITTLE MERRYBELLS
Uvularia sessilifolia
Lily Family

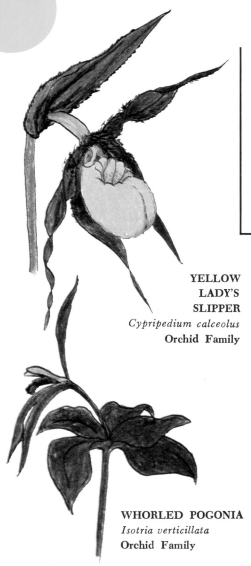

There is only this one species of putty root. It has a single large, strongly ribbed basal leaf which does not grow until late summer. It lasts through the winter but is usually withered away before flowering time. The single flower stalk is from ten to twenty inches high and has from 8 to ten purplish-yellow or greenish-yellow flowers. The whitish lip is crinkly-edged and marked with purple. A quaint name of Adam-and-Eve is given to this plant because of the two underground corms fastened together side-by-side.

YELLOW LADY'S SLIPPER
Cypripedium calceolus
Orchid Family

This golden yellow lady's-slipper is from nine to twenty-seven inches high and grows in rich woods and bogs. The showy inflated lip is nearly two inches long. There are two side petals which are spirally twisted and vary in color from green, to orange, to brown. The hairy stem has from three to five football-shaped leaves which are marked with conspicuous veins which run lengthwise.

SMALL WHORLED POGONIA

Isotria medeoloides

Orchid Family

A smaller pogonia (not shown) differs from the Whorled Pogonia by its relatively short arching sepals. They are not much longer than the petals are. The leaves are less than four inches long and the entire plant is less than ten inches tall.

WHORLED POGONIA
Isotria verticillata
Orchid Family

This member of the orchid family grows in woods from a cluster of hairy roots to a height of from six to fourteen inches. Nearly at the top of the stem is a circle of from five to six elliptic leaves which are attached directly on the main stem. There is a single greenish-yellow flower with three long brownish-purple sepals, each of which is about two inches long. The lateral petals are yellow-green and the lip is green with purplish streaks.

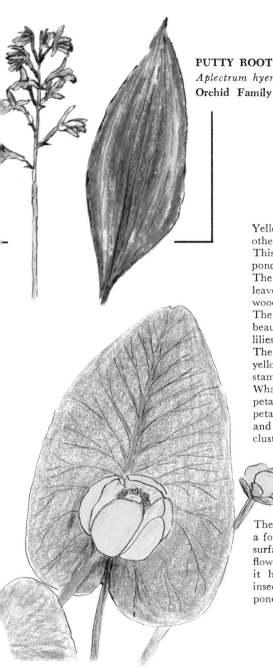

PUTTY ROOT
Aplectrum hyemale
Orchid Family

SPATTERDOCK
Nuphar variegatum
Water Lily Family

Yellow Pond Lily and Cow Lily are other names given to this wild flower. This plant can be found in fresh-water ponds, lakes, and stagnant water holes. The thick round stems, large rounded leaves, and seeds are food for many woodland birds and animals.

The Spatterdock cannot compare in beauty and fragrance to other water lilies — namely the White Water Lily. The big three-inch blooms are bright yellow and have a large core of pistils, stamens and petals in the center.

What appear to be large waxy-yellow petals to the untrained eye, are not petals at all. They are really six sepals and are the same color as the flower cluster itself.

The leaves are very large — often over a foot in length. The leaves float on the surface of the water and protect the flower from waves and wind until it has been fertilized by wind and insects which carry pollen from other pond lilies nearby.

MARSH MARIGOLD
Caltha palustris
Buttercup Family

A more common name in some parts of New England is Cowslip, but this plant is well known to all. It is found growing along streams and brooks, in swamps, marshes, or in wet meadows.

Often the plant is found growing right in swiftly flowing streams. The stem is thick and hollow and the plant often grows to be as high as twenty-four inches.

The Marsh Marigold flower opens in early April before the leaves get too large. The flowers are very waxy looking and are the same color as a buttercup. The flower's ring of yellow

AMERICAN GLOBE-FLOWER
Trollius laxus
Buttercup Family

The American Globe-flower grows in swamps to a height of from one to one and a half feet. Though it is often found in a reclining position, the plant has a single butter-cup-like flower which is at the top of the flowering stem. This flower is at least an inch across and has greenish-yellow sepals which look like petals. The fifteen to twenty-five petals are very tiny and are inside of the ring of broad yellow-green sepals. They appear to be stamens at first glance.

The leaves are very deeply cut and have from five to seven parts. The upper leaves are clasping around the stem and completely surround it.

sepals takes the place of petals. In the center of these shiny yellow sepals, there are many deep yellow stamens. The flower is over an inch across. The plant grows in a clump. The leaves are waxy, heart-shaped, and very shiny. They get larger after the flower fades, and are often gathered to be eaten as greens. The leaves are notched or toothed at the edges.

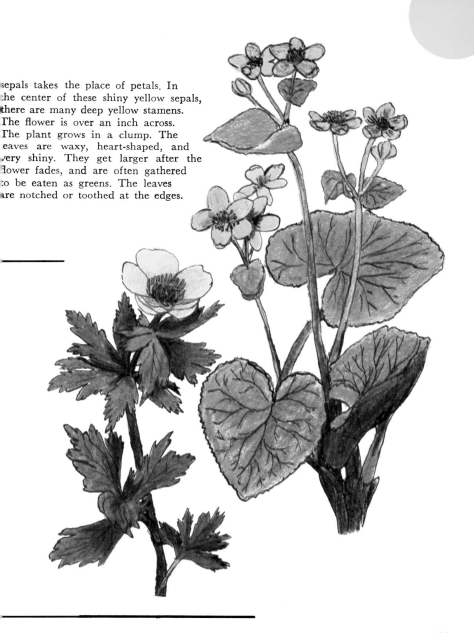

BUTTERCUP
Buttercup Family

There are about thirty-six different species of buttercups in our area, and all are similar to the Common Buttercup drawn on page 140. The distinctive characteristics of four more buttercups are illustrated here.

These shiny yellow flowers love sunshine and may be found in open fields, along lanes, and in marshy places all over the United States.

The buttercup belongs to the crowfoot family. The flower is one inch across and has five yellow petals, five sepals, and many stiff yellow-green stamens which are loaded with pollen.

The leaves are dark green, and are very deeply cut or jagged. The flower should be enjoyed while it is still growing, for soon after it is picked, the petals will fall off.

There are several species of buttercup, but all have the same type of shiny yellow flowers. The leaves differ with each variety. *Swamp Buttercup, Early Buttercup, Hispid Buttercup,* and *Dwarf Buttercup* are some of them. The leaves and stems of the buttercup have a bad taste, so cows and other grass-eating animals will not touch them. Perhaps this explains why the buttercup has remained plentiful while other wild flowers are disappearing.

COMMON BUTTERCUP
Ranunculus acris
Buttercup Family

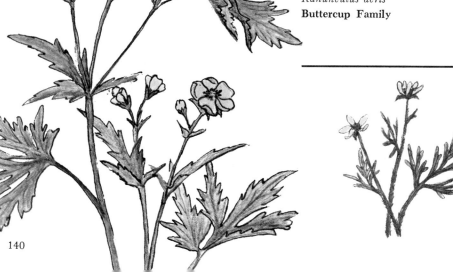

CREEPING BUTTERCUP

Ranunculus repens has long creeping stems which send up erect, hairy branches. The leaves are divided into three long-stalked sections and the leaflets are very deeply cut and toothed. The yellow flowers have from five to nine petals. This buttercup grows in ditches, fields, and wet ground.

SMALL-FLOWERED CROWFOOT or KIDNEYLEAF BUTTERCUP

Ranunculus abortivus has kidney-shaped basal leaves and erect stems that may reach a height of from six to twenty-four inches. The leaves on the stem are divided into narrow, blunt-lobed segments. The insignificant flowers have yellow petals which fold back toward the stem. The center "hump" is yellowish green.

ARLY BUTTERCUP

Ranunculus fascicularis has silky basal aves that are longer than they are ide. The tips of the leaves are not arply pointed but rather bluntly bed. The five to seven petals are arrower than those of most other uttercups. It is the earliest buttercup nd grows in dry woods and prairies a height of from six to twelve inches.

YELLOW-WATER-BUTTERCUP

Ranunculus flabellaris has submerged filament-like leaves and a stout, hollow stem. Usually the plant is submerged in water, but if stranded on a wet shore will grow and form long-stalked leaves with roundish blades that are very deeply cut into from three to five lobes. It is very similar to White Water-Buttercup on page 28.

CELANDINE
Chelidonium majus
Poppy Family

This tall branching flower has leaves which are actually more showy than the flowers. The tip of each branch usually has a loose cluster of buds which bloom one at a time. The flower is bright yellow like a buttercup, but has only four rounded petals. When the petals fall, the pistil in the center grows to a long, slim seed capsule and begins to mature while other buds open and bloom. The thin soft leaves are divided into deeply lobed leaflets with from three to seven leaflets on one leaf. Both the stem and the leaves contain a yellow acrid juice that stains clothes and hands. The flower is abundant on eastern seashores and other wet places, and grows to a height of from one to two feet.

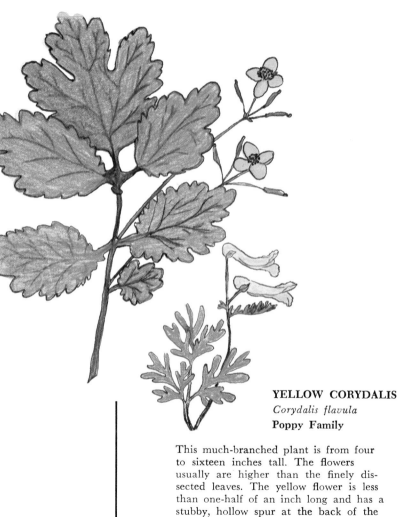

YELLOW CORYDALIS
Corydalis flavula
Poppy Family

This much-branched plant is from four to sixteen inches tall. The flowers usually are higher than the finely dissected leaves. The yellow flower is less than one-half of an inch long and has a stubby, hollow spur at the back of the blossom. The upper petal has a crest which is toothed. Corydalis grows in moist soil of wooded slopes and lowlands.

YELLOW ROCKET
or WINTER CRESS
Barbarea vulgaris
Mustard Family

This member of the mustard family can be easily recognized by its broad shiny upper leaves which are deeply cut and clasp the stem. The bottom leaves have a large end lobe and from two to four side lobes. The stem is very branching and from one to three feet tall. When the four-petaled yellow flowers fade, seed pods appear. These stand erect and close to the stem and are rarely longer than one inch. The beak on the tip of the seed pod is much shorter than that of other mustards. Yellow Rocket grows in wet meadows, fields, and along streams — sometimes making a whole field look yellow.

YELLOW CRESS
Rorippa islandica
Mustard Family

There are several species of Yellow Cress but all are quite similar. Most grow in wet places. The petals are yellow and are very small. The plants are more easily identified by their seed pods which are short and rounded. The species shown in the right-hand corner grows to a height of up to four feet and can be either smooth or hairy. The leaves are very deeply lobed and each lobe is coarsely toothed.

In the left-hand corner is a plant which is similar to Yellow Rocket. The main difference is that the basal leaves have more side lobes than the Rocket. Often there are up to ten pairs of lobes on each leaf. The mature seed pods are much longer than those on the Rocket and may be as long as three inches.

EARLY
WINTER CRESS
Barbarea verna
Mustard Family

WILD RADISH or
JOINTED CHARLOCK
Raphanus raphanistrum
Mustard Family

This member of the mustard family
has a coarse, purple, bristly stem and
deeply lobed leaves with a large
rounded lobe at the end. The four-
petaled flowers are pale yellow or
whitish and are marked with showy
lilac-colored veins.
The seed pod is noticeably beaded
when it is mature. Jointed Charlock
grows in waste places, sandy soil, and
in vacant lots to a height of
from one to two and one-half feet.

CHARLOCK
Brassica kaber
Mustard Family

The distinguishing characteristics of this
mustard are the leaves and the pods.
The rest of the plant is similar to
those above. The leaves *are not* deeply
lobed to the midrib, as leaves
above are. The long, thin, seed pod
has flat surfaces and ridges on it and
is not beaded. The beak is about
one-third to one-half as long as
the mature pod and has four flat sides.

145

WHITE MUSTARD
Brassica herta
Mustard Family

At the right is part of the White Mustard plant. It can be distinguished from other mustards by the bristly pods which end in a flattened beak which is often as large as or larger than the pod itself. White Mustard is a stiff, hairy plant which grows from one to two feet tall in fields and in waste places.

BLACK MUSTARD
Brassica nigra
Mustard Family

As on the other mustards, the flowers on the Black Mustard open first at the bottom of the spike. Small erect seed pods which closely hug the stem replace the flowers as new flowers farther up the spike start to open. The stem lengthens as new flowers open at the top. The basal leaves are shiny green and have a large end lobe with two pairs of smaller lobes. The top leaves on the stem are not lobed — only toothed.

BARREN STRAWBERRY
Waldsteinia fragarioides
Rose Family

This plant grows on wooded hillsides to a height of three to eight inches.

It resembles a strawberry plant, except the flowers are yellow. The leaves are toothed and three-parted like those of a strawberry, but are more blunt at the tips. The fruit resembles a dried strawberry. It is not juicy like a berry and is not edible.

146

HEDGE MUSTARD
Sisymbrium officinale
Mustard Family

This is a common weed which grows in most of the United States and Europe. The plant blooms very early in the spring and grows larger as warmer weather comes.

The flowers are very similar to those of Black Mustard, but they are much smaller. They are the same color yellow and have four petals, but they are less than 1/5 inch wide.

When the flowers go by, seed pods about 1/2 inch in length form and are closely pressed to the stem of the plant. The clusters of flowers continue to form as the stem lengthens and the seed pods form.

The leaves are much longer than those of the Black Mustard. They are more angular and are deeply lobed and deeply toothed than those of Black Mustard. On some plants there will be two or four long teeth on each leaf at the base where it is attached to the stem.

Indian Strawberry has a creeping stem from which leaves and flowerstalks arise. The leaf is three-parted and similar to those of a strawberry. The yellow flower differs from those on a cinquefoil by having five bracts alternating with the five sepals on the back of the flower. The green bracts are three-toothed at the broad tip, and are longer than the petals and the sepals. The fruit is juicy and berry-like, but it is inedible.

INDIAN STRAWBERRY
Duchesnea indica
Rose Family

SILVERWEED
Potentilla
anserina
Rose Family

This spreading cinquefoil spreads by reddish runners which take root and send up erect leaves and flowers on separate stalks. The leaves have numerous, sharply toothed segments, often as many as twenty or more on one leaf rib. The underside is silky with long silvery white hairs. The enlarged underside of the leaflet shows detail. Silverweed grows on wet, sandy or rocky shores.

Rough Avens grows on low ground dry woods and rocky places to a height of from fifteen to thirty inch The stems are hairy and the large, hairy leaves are divided into thr toothed leaflets — the middle be larger than the other two. The peta are pale yellow or cream-colored an the green sepals are larger than the petals. The fruit is a hard, brown oval or round head covered with bristly hairs.

CINQUEFOIL
Rose Family

There are many cinquefoils and a have the same general characterist There are five petals (usually yellow and five sepals which show between the petals. The stamens and pistil are numerous and form a "hump" i the center. Cinquefoil means "five leaves" and most of the cinquefoil have five finger-like leaves.

COMMON CINQUEFOIL
Rose Family

Potentilla simplex is at the bottom the page. It has stems that rest on the ground and take root at the no to send up new growth. The leaf blades on this plant have curved sid and teeth which continue nearly to the base, but other than this one difference, it is very similar to Dwarf Cinquefoil.

Potentilla canadensis is below on left. It grows in dry soil, fields, and woods to a height of about four or five inches. The stem is erect at first, but then arches and rests on the ground. It has five-parted wedge-shaped leaf blades with straight sides and teeth only above the middle. The stems have dense silver hair.

Rose Family

CINQUEFOIL
DWARF

Potentilla recta is below. It grows in fields and along roads and is a very hairy branching plant. The leaflets are in groups of five or seven. The flowers are larger than those of other cinquefoils and are in a flat terminal cluster. Each petal is perfectly heart-shaped and the entire blossom may be as large as an inch across.

Rose Family
CINQUEFOIL
ROUGH-FRUITED

SILVERY CINQUEFOIL
Rose Family

Potentilla argentea is in the middle. It has branching stems and may be nearly two feet tall. The five-part leaf segments are narrow and have teeth similar to those of an oak leaf. The edges often roll inward and the underside has silvery wool on it. The flowers are less than one-half inch across and are in clusters at the ends of white wooly branches.

ROUGH
CINQUEFOIL
Rose Family

Potentilla norvegica at the bottom suggests a yellow-flowered strawberry plant, but is much taller. It is a stout, bushy plant up to three feet tall. The leaves and stem are usually hairy. The leaves are in groups of three instead of five and are coarsely toothed. The flowers are about one-half inch across and the petals are slightly shorter than the green sepals which can easily be seen between the petals.

YELLOW
HOP CLOVER
Trifolium
agrarium
Pea Family

Hop Clover grows erect and up to eighteen inches tall in waste places and along roadsides. The small leaflets are in sets of three and have very short leaf stalks or are attached directly to the stem itself. The yellow flowers are arranged in a cylinder-shaped cluster at the end of the stem. As the flowers fade, the individual flowers turn brown and fold downward. This brown head looks similar to that of dried hops — hence the name of Hop Clover.

Indigo is a smooth plant with numerous leaves in sets of three leaflets. They are gray-green in color and are often attached right on the main stem. The stem and leaves often have a bluish bloom on them. The leaves turn black when dried. The numerous pea-like, yellow flowers are in loose flower clusters at the ends of the branches.

WILD INDIGO
Baptisia tinctoria
Pea Family

YELLOW
SWEET-CLOVER
Meliotus officinalis
Pea Family

This tall bushy clover found along roadsides and in waste places grows to a height of from two to five feet. The leaves are divided into sets of three leaflets. The bright yellow flowers are arranged in numerous spike-like racemes which grow from leaf axils. This sweet-clover gives off an odor of new-mown hay.

BLACK MEDIC
Medicago lupulina
Pea Family

This common weed has downy stems which rest on the ground. It grows in waste lands, on lawns, and along roadsides. The leaves are in sets of three leaflets that are either blunt or have a tiny spine at the tip. The yellow flowers are in almost round flower heads, but are quickly replaced by clusters of twisted black seed pods.

This is a hairy plant with large two-colored, sweet pea-like flowers. The standard is yellow and the wings are pink. The leaves are divided into many pairs of leaflets with a single leaflet at the end. There are from nine to fifteen leaflets on each stem. Goat's Rue grows in sandy woods to a height of from one to two feet.

GOAT'S RUE
Tephrosia virginiana
Pea Family

Gorse is a dense, spiny, much-branched shrub from two to six feet tall which grows in sandy soil of waste places. It has no true leaves (except, possibly, on early new growth), but has long slender spines instead. Every branch ends in spiny tips. The bright flowers are in panicles at the ends of branches. They grow on short stems (pedicels) in the axils of the spikes. Two hairy sepals are below each flower, and the ridge on the under part of the lower petal is also hairy.

GORSE
Ulex europeus
Pea Family

BROOM
or SCOTCH BROOM
Cytisus scoparius
Pea Family

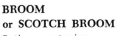

Broom is a bushy shrub which grows from three to five feet tall in sandy soil of roadsides, pine barrens, or sea coast. It has stiff, slender branches and stems with angles or ridges. The small lower leaves are in sets of three, but sometimes the tiny upper leaves are attached singly to the stem. The largest part of the leaf is nearest to the tip, rather than the base. The bright yellow flowers have two toothed lips and are often as long as an inch. They are in long racemes at the top of the plant.

151

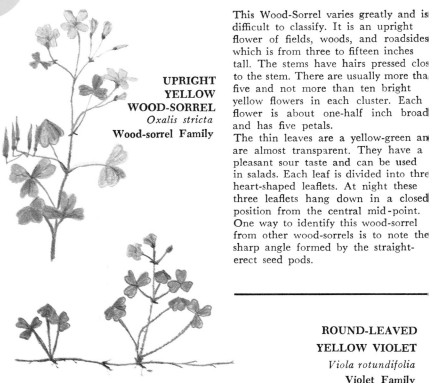

**UPRIGHT
YELLOW
WOOD-SORREL**
Oxalis stricta
Wood-sorrel Family

This Wood-Sorrel varies greatly and is difficult to classify. It is an upright flower of fields, woods, and roadsides which is from three to fifteen inches tall. The stems have hairs pressed clos to the stem. There are usually more tha five and not more than ten bright yellow flowers in each cluster. Each flower is about one-half inch broad and has five petals.

The thin leaves are a yellow-green an are almost transparent. They have a pleasant sour taste and can be used in salads. Each leaf is divided into thre heart-shaped leaflets. At night these three leaflets hang down in a closed position from the central mid-point. One way to identify this wood-sorrel from other wood-sorrels is to note the sharp angle formed by the straight-erect seed pods.

**CREEPING
WOOD-SORREL**
Oxalis repens
Wood-sorrel Family

This oxalis is very similar to the one above but it has creeping stems. It is more hairy, and the hairs are not pressed close to the stem as in the above plant.

**ROUND-LEAVED
YELLOW VIOLET**
Viola rotundifolia
Violet Family

Another common name for this plant is the Early Yellow Violet. It grows in cool, rich woods to a height of from two to five inches. The petals ar bright yellow; the two side ones are bearded; and the three lower one are marked with brown lines. The small roundish or heart-shaped leaves are very close to the ground below th flowers. This is called a "stemless" violet because the leaves and flowers rise directly from the ground on separate stalks. This violet — as wit

152

DOWNY YELLOW VIOLET
Viola pubescens
Violet Family

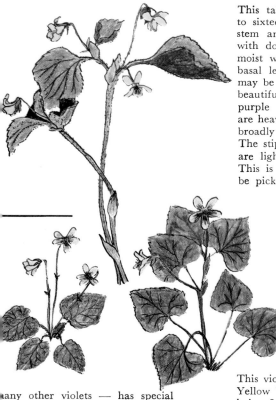

This tall forking violet is from eight to sixteen inches tall and has a stem and leaves which are covered with downy soft hairs. It grows in moist woodlands. Usually there are no basal leaves, but occasionally there may be a single one. The flowers are a beautiful clear yellow and have purple stripes. The two lateral petals are heavily bearded. The leaves are broadly heart-shaped and are toothed. The stipules at the base of the leaves are light colored, pointed, and large. This is one violet which should not be picked freely.

SMOOTH YELLOW VIOLET
Viola pensylvanica
Violet Family

...any other violets — has special ...owers called cleistogamous flowers ...hich remain hidden and never open. ...ithin these flowers, seeds develop ...nd are dispersed for the next year's ...owers. For this reason, most stemless ...olets are not in danger of ...xtermination and may be freely picked.

This violet is similar to the Downy Yellow Violet but is smaller and is not hairy. It grows in moist woods and low meadows. There are from one to five long-stalked basal leaves which are broadly heart-shaped. The stems are smooth and brownish and contain smaller heart-shaped leaves. The petals are bright yellow with purplish veins. The side petals have tufts of hair.

GOLDEN HEATHER
Hudsonia ericoides
Rockrose Family

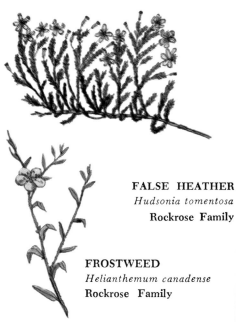

This low, bushy plant forms dense mats up to two feet across on dry gravelly soil or on rocks. It is from o to eight inches tall and is a dry-looking, bushy, brownish plant with yellow flowers. It has spreading needl like leaves. It has vivid yellow flowers which bloom in a great mass and often conceal the mat of leaves and stems below. The flowers are about one-fourth inch across, have a hairy ovary, and have five rounded notche petals.

False Heather (not shown) is very similar to the above, but is not a green. It grows only in sand of dun and beaches, has a grayer scale-like leaf, and pale yellow blossoms at the twig tips. It is a shrubby plant and is often covered with whitish hairs.

FALSE HEATHER
Hudsonia tomentosa
Rockrose Family

FROSTWEED
Helianthemum canadense
Rockrose Family

Frostweed usually has only one main stem. The flower grows at the top of this stem, but soon smaller, side branches will grow taller than the flower. Usually there is one flower and one main stem, but occasionally a plant with a few stems and two flowers may be found. It is a foot or more tall and has narrow pointed alternate leaves. The stem and leaves are hairy. The yellow flower has five large, over-lapping petals and many stamens. It is about one inch across. Later in the season, clusters of flowers without petals appear on branches, are fertilized, but do not open. As fall approaches, the bark on the stem may split and release tiny strings of ice crystals, hence the English name of Frostweed.

SUNDROPS
Oenothera perennis
Evening Primrose Family

This plant grows along trails, roads, and in fields or open woods to a height of from two to three feet. The leaves are very numerous and are arranged in pairs. They have blunt tips and small holes or perforations scattered in them. The bright yellow flowers are arranged in a rather tight terminal cluster. Each star-shaped flower is about one inch across and has five petals with black-dotted margins.

**COMMON
ST. JOHNSWORT**
Hypericum perforatum
St. Johnswort Family

This plant grows in dry fields, open woods, and along roadsides to a height of from one to three feet. The flower has bright yellow rays that are notched at the tips. The center is brownish or purple-brown and becomes more conical in shape as the flower ades. The leaves are covered with white hairs on both sides. They are placed alternately on the hairy stem.

**BLACK-EYED
SUSAN**
*Rudbeckia
hirta*
**Composite
Family**

This day-blooming flower has blossoms similar to those of the Evening Primrose only smaller. The buds at the top are in a drooping position, but straighten upright when blooming. The stems are erect or spreading and are from ten to twenty-four inches tall. The light green leaves are linear or lance-shaped and have untoothed margins. They either have a short leaf stem or are attached directly to the stem by an enlargement at the leaf base. The stem is downy with short hairs and is reddish at leaf axils. The four-petaled yellow flower has two small sepals which are joined at the tip. These fold back when the flower blooms and give the appearance of a single heart-shaped sepal. The flower has a structure called hypanthium and an inferior ovary. This means that the male parts (stamens) are above the petals and the female parts are below the petals. The ovary is the long ribbed capsule in the axils of the leaves.

**EVENING
PRIMROSE**
Oenothera biennis
Evening Primrose Family

Evening Primrose grows in fields, waste places, and along roadsides to a height of from one to five feet. The flowers have four broad yellow petals and a cross-shaped stigma in the center. The individual flowers are nearly two inches broad but usually close when exposed to bright sunlight. The flowers last only over night and new buds open in the morning. The long sepals are turned backwards towards the stem. The narrow, hairy leaves are alternate on the hairy stem. The stem is green, but turns reddish as the flower matures.

PINESAP
Monotropa hypopithys
Heath Family

This plant looks similar to the Indian Pipe, but has several dull yellow nodding flowers at the tip instead of only one. It is not white as is the Indian Pipe. The entire plant is yellow, tan, or sometimes pale pink in color. It is quite hairy and grows in open or sandy woods. It is from three to twelve inches high. The stems have crowded scales which are up to one-half inch long. The upper scales are sometimes toothed. The dull yellow flowers at the tip usually have five parts, but the ones nearer the stem sometimes have only three or four petals. The petals are from three-fourths to one inch long and are slightly hairy.

FRINGED LOOSESTRIFE
Steironema ciliatum
Primrose Family

This is the same plant which some authors call Lysimachia ciliata. It grow in swamps, wet thickets, and on stream banks in full sun. It is often branched at the top, and reaches a height of from one to four feet. The yellow flowers have five fringed or toothed petals, and frequently face downward. The paired leaves have ha on their leaf stems.

SQUAW-ROOT
Conopholis americana
Broomrape Family

This plant has tan colored tight-fitting scales which are so stiff the plant resembles a pinecone. The plant is from three to eight inches tall and grows in rich woods in groups at the base of trees — especially oak trees. The plant lacks green leaves so is unable to make its own food. It is a parasite and lives off the food of other plant There are many uneven pale yellow flowers which are about one-half of a inch long. The top part of the flower forms a hood over the stamens and three lobed lower petals. The irregula flowers protrude from between the stiff scales at the top of the plant.

Swamp Candles is also known as Bulb-bearing Loosestrife. It grows in marshes, swampy spots or moist thickets

SWAMP CANDLES or YELLOW LOOSESTRIFE
Lysimachia terrestris
Primrose Family

and is from eight to twenty inches tall. The leaves, which are opposite each other on the stem, are long and pointed and are sometimes dotted with black. Often, little branches with more leaves will grow from the axils of the leaves after the flowers have begun to fade.

The flowers are about one-third of an inch wide and are arranged in a tall slender raceme at the end of the stem. Each flower has five yellow petals which have a ring of red or purple dots at the base of each petal. The pistil is easily seen protruding from the center of the ring of yellow petals.

WHORLED LOOSESTRIFE
Lysimachia quadrifolia
Primrose Family

This loosestrife has star-like yellow flowers which are similar to the other two, but both the leaves and the flowers are arranged in whorls of four at regular intervals on the stem.
Whorled Loosestrife grows in woods and thickets to a height of from one to three feet, but it usually is about eighteen inches tall.

Meadow Parsnip is a sparingly branch
plant of dry woods, thickets, or banks.
The toothed, stem-leaves are divided
into three leaflets and the top ones
are attached directly to the main
stem. The broad basal leaves are eith
heart-shaped or round. This species
can be easily distinguished from the or
above by the mature fruit. In Golden
Alexander, the fruits are ribbed,
but in this species, the fruits are winge
There is both a purple-flowered and
a yellow-flowered variety of this plan

HOARY PUCCOON

Lithospermum canescens

Forget-Me-Not Family

The Hoary Puccoon is found in open
woods, on plains, and in dry sandy soil.
It is from six to twenty inches tall and
has curled-over clusters of yellow or
orange flowers. Each individual flower
has five flat lobes which form into a
tube that hides the stamens. The
small flower is about one-half of an inch
long and in terminal leafy racemes. The
leaves are very slender and are
alternate on the stem. The stem and
leaves are covered with stiff hairs.

HAIRY PUCCOON

Lithospermum croceum

Forget-Me-Not Family

This plant is larger and stouter than
the one above, but is very similar. The
flowers are larger and the corolla-tube
is bearded at the base.

MEADOW PARSNIP

Thaspium trifoliatum

Parsley Family

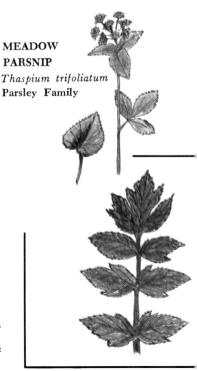

GOLDEN ALEXANDER or EARLY MEADOW PARSNIP
Zizia aurea
Parsley Family

Golden Alexander is a branching flower which grows in wet thickets, swamps, and moist fields to a height of from one to two feet. The petals are bright yellow and are arranged in a wheel-like compound umbel. The rays of the umbel are nearly the same length, and there may be as many as twenty small umbels. Each leaf is divided into three parts and each part is divided into three deeply-toothed, pointed leaflets with conspicuous veins.

YELLOW PIMPERNEL
Taenidia integerrima
Parsley Family

WILD PARSNIP
Pastinaca sativa
Parsley Family

This is the largest of the four pictured. It can be distinguished by its immenseness — sometimes as tall as five feet. It has a stout, deeply grooved stem and large leaves. The leaves are divided into from five to fifteen sharply toothed leaflets. It is a weed found in vacant lots, along dry roadsides, and in waste places.

This branching plant is from one to three feet tall and grows in dry woods, rocky thickets, and hillsides. It is similar to the two above, but can be distinguished by the untoothed leaflets and the slender, smooth stem with a whitish bloom on it.

159

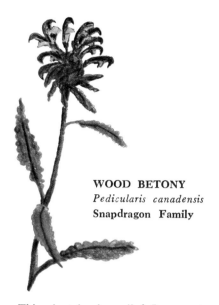

WOOD BETONY
Pedicularis canadensis
Snapdragon Family

BUTTER-AND-EGGS
Linaria vulgaris
Snapdragon Family

This member of the Snapdragon
family is also known as Toadflax in
some areas of New England. It is
found growing along roads, in dry
fields, waste places, and gravel pits.
Its height varies from one to three
feet depending upon the type of soil.
The leaves are very numerous and
are placed alternately around the
stem. The snap-dragon-like flowers
are of two shades of yellow and grow
in long spikes at the end of the
flower stalk. The corolla is pale
yellow with an orange-yellow inflated
center. The top and bottom petals
are closed into a throat and there
is a long narrow spur hanging down
from the back of each flower.

This plant is also called Lousewort,
Early Pedicularis, or Beefsteak Plant.
At one time, this plant was thought
to be the source of lice in grazing
animals. It grows in both dry woods
and wet sunny meadows and is from
four to eighteen inches tall.
The long soft leaves are deeply lobed
and hairy. They are alternately
scattered along the stem and are also
at the base of the plant. The leaves
are somewhat fern-like, and are
often bronze or reddish colored.
The plant is topped with a close
cluster or whorl of short tubular
dragonmouth flowers. The hooded
flowers vary in color from pale yellow
to wine red, but usually have some
brown on them. Underneath the
cluster of flowers, there are many
smaller leaf-like bracts.
Wood Betony often lives off the
plants around it and is called a
parasite — though it is capable of
making its own food.

YELLOW RATTLE
Rhinanthus crista-galli
Snapdragon Family

Yellow Rattle grows in old fields, waste places, and thickets to a height of from eight to twenty-four inches. It may have either a simple or a branching stem. The stem is four-sided and only two of the sides have hair on them. The flower has two lips. The upper lip is rounded and has teeth on the underside. The lower lip is divided into three lobes. The flower is mostly yellow, but sometimes the teeth of the upper lip are a darker color and sometimes there are dark spots on the lower lip. The flower is in a sac-like calyx which becomes more inflated as seeds form inside. The seeds will rattle when the plant is moved — hence the name of Yellow Rattle. The leaves are in pairs along the stem and have toothed edges.

COMMON MULLEIN
Verbascum thapsus
Snapdragon Family

This gray-green wooly plant grows in waste places, fields, and along roadsides to a height of from two to six feet. It has a stout erect stem and large, thick, felt-like leaves that grow right into the stem. The saucer-shaped flowers are in a thick, club-like raceme. They have five yellow petals and are covered on the backside with whitish hairs.

The Bladderwort is rooted in shallow water of slow-moving streams, ponds or bogs. The stems are aquatic and horizontally submerged branches go out from the base of the flower stalk. The leaves are densely arranged alternately along separate leafstalks. There are no bladders among the leaf segments, but other rootlike leaves bear several large bladders. The naked flower-bearing scape is about eight inches high and bears from one to four yellow flowers that look similar to a snapdragon. The upper lip is triangular and about one-third of an inch broad. The bottom lip is a little larger and the spur is clearly visible.

This Bladderwort has only a few small inconspicuous grass-like leaves which are embedded in the mud of bogs or sandy shores. The flower scape is brown and is from two to thirteen inches tall. There are from one to five bright yellow, fragrant flowers with a long spur hanging down. The low lip of the flower is nearly two-thirds of an inch long and has a hood-like top part over it.

HORNED BLADDERWORT
Utricularia cornuta
Bladderwort Family

COMMON or GREATER BLADDERWORT
Utricularia vulgaris
Bladderwort Family

FLAT-LEAVED BLADDERWORT
Utricularia intermedia
Bladderwort Family

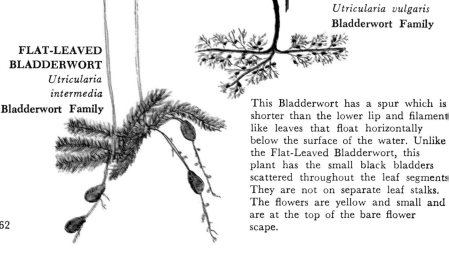

This Bladderwort has a spur which is shorter than the lower lip and filament like leaves that float horizontally below the surface of the water. Unlike the Flat-Leaved Bladderwort, this plant has the small black bladders scattered throughout the leaf segments. They are not on separate leaf stalks. The flowers are yellow and small and are at the top of the bare flower scape.

HONEYSUCKLE
Honeysuckle Family

There are many honeysuckles and from a distance they all look like a bushy, branching plant. Three are given here.

NORTHERN BUSH-HONEYSUCKLE

Diervilla lonicera is from one to four feet tall and grows in dry or rocky soil in woods openings or at the edges of fields. This is the only honeysuckle with *toothed leaves*. The leafblades are oblong and pointed at the tip and are opposite each other on the stem. The trumpet-shaped flowers are pale yellow and grow in sets of twos or threes from the leaf axils and at the tips of the stems. The stamens protrude noticeably, and the petals fold way back.

FLY-HONEYSUCKLE

NORTHERN FLY-HONEYSUCKLE

Lonicera canadensis is shown enlarged in the accompanying illustration so that the distinctive characteristics may be seen. The funnel-shaped flower is yellowish, but the petals do not fold back as in the one above. There is a sack-like "hump" on one side of the base of the flower. The flowers are in pairs on a single flower stem (pedicel) but the *ovaries are separate* below the flowers. The leaves are rather blunt and oblong and the ripe berries are red.

Lonicera villosa is enlarged so it can be distinguished from the one at the left in two ways. First, there is no sack-like hump on the base of the flowers. Second, The *ovaries are united* into one barrel-shaped structure instead of two separate structures as in the species above. There are two long, linear, green bracts under the ovaries and the ripe berries are blue.

COMMON
SOW-THISTLE
Sonchus oleraceus
Composite Family

This troublesome weed has smooth bracts and stems and sometimes grows to be six or more feet tall. The leaf margins sometimes have weak bristles. The lower leaves are deeply cut but the top leaves are merely toothed. There are large, prickly, rounded or pointed "ears" at the base of the leaf which surround the stem. The small insignificant flowers are in small heads of yellow ray flowers.

YELLOW THISTLE
Cirsium horridulum
Composite Family

BLESSED
THISTLE
Cnicus benedictus
Composite Family

This wooly yellow thistle is native to our area and grows to a height of from one to four feet. It grows in open places, especially in salt marshes and on sandy coastal shores.
The leaves are very deeply cut and have extremely sharp bristles.
The flower is usually yellow and is surrounded by a circle of prickly leaf-like bracts. These bracts are soft tipped.

This branching hairy thistle has a deep yellow head made up of tiny, perfect, tubular flowers. Surrounding the yellow head are large spine-tipped leaf bracts. The flower heads are at the end of the branches. The leaves along the hairy stem are alternate and toothed — but not spiny like the leaves on the Yellow Thistle.

164

KING DEVIL
Hieracium pratense
Composite Family

RATTLESNAKE WEED
Hieracium venosum
Composite Family

This plant is similar to hawkweeds but may be easily identified by the reddish or purple veining on the green leaves. The elliptical basal leaves have long hairs and the underside is often purplish or reddish. The smooth stem (or stems) is from one to two and one-half feet tall and is usually branching at the top. There are numerous yellow flowering heads at the top — sometimes as many as forty flowers on a large plant. The green bracts holding the heads are not hairy. It grows in open woods and clearings.

This plant is similar to a Devil's Paintbrush only it is yellow. King Devil is from one to three feet tall and grows in fields and along roadsides. The stems and bracts under the flower heads are covered with black, bristly hairs. The stem sometimes has a few tiny reduced leaves, but usually it is leafless. The narrow basal leaves are from two to ten inches long and taper as they reach the stem. The leaves are hairy on both sides. There are numerous yellow flower heads at the top of the stem.

165

YELLOW GOAT'S BEARD
Tragopogon pratensis
Composite Family

Goat's Beard grows in fields, waste places,
and along roads to a height of
eight inches to three feet. It has
narrow grass-like leaves which clasp
the smooth stem. Below the pale
yellow flower heads are long, pointed
bracts. These lengthen and turn
backwards as the flower goes to seed.
When in seed, the head is round
and looks similar to the seed head
of a dandelion only is much larger,
and is more delicate.

PINEAPPLE WEE
Matricaria matricarioi
Composite Fam

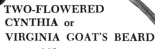

TWO-FLOWERED CYNTHIA or VIRGINIA GOAT'S BEARD
Krigia biflora
Composite Family

This Goat's Beard grows in moist
woods, fields, and along roadsides
to a height of from eight to
thirty-two inches. There are from
one to six yellow-orange flowering
heads on a smooth, divided stem.
Most commonly, only two flowers
will be on a plant, one on each part
of the forked stem. The basal leaves
have long petioles and are varied in
size and shape. They may be either
smooth, jagged, toothed, or lobed
like those of a dandelion.
There is usually only one upper leaf
which embraces the smooth flower stalk.
Circling the yellow flower head are
from nine to eighteen upright green,
pointed bracts. As the flower ages,
these bracts turn backward.

166

This branching, leafy plant grows in farm yards, along roadsides, and in waste places to a height of from six to eighteen inches. The leaves are a deep yellow-green and are deeply cut and re-cut. When the plant is bruised, it emits an odor similar to a pineapple.

The yellow-green flowers are in conical or pointed heads with green bracts surrounding the base of the head. There are not any rays as there are on most other members of this family.

SNEEZEWEED YARROW

Achillea ptarmica

Composite Family

This plant grows in damp roadsides, beaches, and fields to a height of from one to two feet. It has long pointed leaves with saw-toothed edges which alternate on the stem. From the axils of these leaves, new stems with more leaves occur. The flower heads, from one-half to three-fourths across, have yellow centers, and whitish-yellow rays.

ROUNDLEAF RAGWORT

Senecio obovatus

Composite Family

This ragwort is smaller — about six inches to two feet and the flowering stems arise from slender runners. It grows in rocky woods or on shaded banks. The basal leaves are oval and have toothed margins. The blade is widest above the middle and tapers to a slender stalk as it reaches the stem. The young leaves may have tufts of wool on them.

This ragwort resembles the one below, but the blades of the basal leaves are different. The blade is either a long oval or a long arrowhead shape with a pointed tip. Some of the larger leaves have a few ragged lobes on each side of the midrib. The flowers are very similar, but are paler in color.

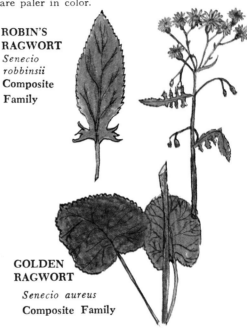

ROBIN'S RAGWORT
Senecio robbinsii
Composite Family

GOLDEN RAGWORT
Senecio aureus
Composite Family

This ragwort is from one to three feet in height and grows mostly in wet places. The daisy-like flower heads are about three-fourths of an inch across and have from eight to twelve yellow ray flowers on each head. The narrow stem leaves are deeply cut but the basal leaves are either heart-shaped or egg-shaped with toothed edges. The broad basal leaves have long leaf stalks and are sometimes reddish on the underside. The entire plant is smooth when it is mature — but is apt to be somewhat hairy during early growth.

167

CAROLINA DWARF DANDELION
Krigia virginica
Composite Family

This is a small, slender dandelion
with a single yellow blossom
which looks like a hawkweed flower.
The head is much smaller — about one-
half inch broad — and there are no
reflexed outer bracts at the bottom
of the head. Instead of the bracts, there
are scales and bristles. The leaves in
the whorl at the base are usually not

RED-SEEDED DANDELION
Taraxacum erythrospermum
Composite Family

This dandelion differs in several
ways from the common
Dandelion. It has smaller heads, red
seeds, leaves that are narrower and
more deeply cut, and the green bracts
at the base of the flower head are
pointed out instead of being curved
backwards. This Dandelion grows in dry
fields and is from two to eight inches
tall.

all alike. The early spring leaves are
often entire and not toothed, while
those that develop later do have the
dandelion-like toothed leaves. Sometimes
the plant becomes branched later in
the season.

The dandelion is probably the best-
known of all wild flowers. It grows in
fields and on lawns in nearly every
country in the world. Though it is
considered to be a pest by most people
who have lawns, the leaves may be
cooked as greens, the blossom is
delicious when dipped in batter and
fried, medicine is made from its roots,
and wine is made from its flowers.
The narrow green leaves with jagged
edges are attached to the root. Buds
form in the center and then rise on
milky, hollow stems and open to form
a shiny golden head. There are
reflexed outer bracts at the base of
the flower head. The flower head is
actually made up of many perfect
flowers in one golden head. When these

yellow heads dry up, a white puffball
forms. A breeze — or a delighted
child's puff — will scatter these seeds
in all directions like
little parachutes.

COMMON DANDELION
Taraxacum officinale
Composite Family

COLTSFOOT
Tussilago farfara
Composite Family

There is only one species of Coltsfoot. Coltsfoot has a long horizontal underground stem which, in early spring, sends forth a stalk with reddish scales. A single bristly yellow flower head with an orange center is formed at the tip. The rays are in layers. Large roundish, indented leaves appear after the flowers fade. The leaves have white hairs on underside. The stem is from six to eighteen inches tall. Coltsfoot can be found growing in waste places, on railroad banks, and on the edges of roads.

LAMB SUCCORY
Arnoseris minima
Composite Family

This member of the composite family is easily identified by the swollen stem below the yellow flower heads. The flowers have very short, flat rays and the leaves are very coarsely toothed. It grows to a height of from six to fourteen inches along roads or in sandy waste places.

T'S-EAR
pochoeris radicata
mposite Family

Cat's-Ear has yellow dandelion-like heads about an inch wide. It grows on lawns and in other grassy areas. The stem is from eight to sixteen inches tall and has scale-like bracts scattered along it. On some plants, the stem is forked; on others the stem is simple. The bracts under the flower head are of different lengths and overlap each other. There is a circle of leaves at the base. The leaves are very jagged and densely covered with hairs.

COMMON GROUNDSEL
Senecio vulgaris
Composite Family

This branching, leafy "weed" grows from six inches to two feet in height and has soft thick leaves which are coarsely toothed. It is similar to the ragworts on page 167, but the flower does not have the showy, flat, yellow rays of the ragwort. The stem and leaves are smooth. The outer bracts under the yellow flower head are tipped with black.

169

This plant with grass-like leaves is from one to five feet tall and grows along streams, at edges of ponds, and in swamps. The flower-bearing stem is flat and is very similar to the leaves. The green spathe grows from the top of this stem and looks like a flat, green extension of the stem itself. The spadix, which is covered with the tiny flowers, juts out at an angle from the main stem. The minute flowers form a diamond pattern on the narrow spadix. The tiny flowers are perfect and are yellowish-brown.

Green Dragon has solitary leaves which are divided into from five fifteen leaflets. The plant is from one to four feet tall and grows in rich woods and along streams. The flowers are very tiny and are crowd at the base of the spadix which ha a long yellow-green tapering poin The tapering point is often called t "dragon's snout" and is from four to eight inches long. The green spath covers the flowers. It is pointed, t but not nearly as long as the spadi The mature berries are reddish-orange in color.

SWEET FLAG
Acorus calamus
Arum Family

GREEN DRAGO
or DRAGON AR
Arisaema dracontium
Arum Family

JACK-IN-THE-PULPIT

Arisaema atrorubens
Arum Family

This wild flower could not have been given a better name, for it looks like a little minister in a pulpit about to preach a sermon. Though he looks like a minister, he is actually a murderer, for he catches insects which can not climb out the slippery insides of the "pulpit." There are quite a few species of Jack-in-the-Pulpits, but they all have the same general appearance. Jack is called the spadix and the hood is the spathe. The true flowers are clustered together at the very base of the spadix and can not be seen unless the "pulpit" is pulled apart. The plant grows to be from ten inches to three feet, depending upon the amount of moisture and the richness of the soil. The beautiful compound leaves are much taller than Jack himself. Each leaf is divided into three smaller leaflets. In late June or early July, Jack and his hood dry up and leave a cluster of red berries. The Indians of New England used to use these berries as food and boiled the root. The root is shaped like a small turnip, so some call this plant Indian Turnip.

This wild flower is a member of the Arum family, as is the Skunk Cabbage, the Wild Calla, and the Jack-in-the-Pulpit. This is a fairly large family of plants, many of which grow around the water. All of them have small flowers crowded around the bottom of the spadix and usually covered or protected by a spathe. The Green Arrow-Arum is a large flower which often grows right in the water of lakes and streams. The plant is often one and one-half feet high. The green pointed spathe grows about five inches long. If this spathe is pulled apart, the long green spadix with tiny flowers clustered at the bottom may be seen.

The leaves are shaped like an Indian Arrowhead — hence the name. These leaves sometimes grow to be twenty inches long. The berries, which develop at the base of the spadix, are green.

GREAT SOLOMON'S SEAL
Polygonatum canaliculatum
Lily Family

Great Solomon's Seal is a taller and coarser plant than the one at the right. It grows in rich woods, thickets, and along rivers to a height of from two to five feet. It has arching stems with alternate leaves. Greenish white flowers hang in clusters with from one to fifteen flowers in a cluster, usually five or six.

GREEN
ARROW-ARUM
Peltandra virginica
Arum Family

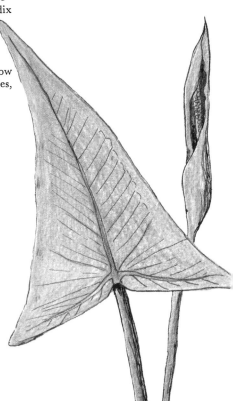

SOLOMON'S SEAL
Polygonatum biflorum
Lily Family

This Solomon's Seal has pairs of
bell-like yellowish green flowers that
dangle from the axils of the leaves.
The leaves are alternate on the stem
and have veins which go lengthwise.
It grows in moist woods and thickets
to a height of from one to three
feet. See page 134 in the yellow
section for further details.

HAIRY SOLOMON'S SEAL
Polygonatum pubescens
Lily Family

This Solomon's Seal is very similar
to the others shown above, but there
are hairs along the veins on the
underside of the leaf. The erect,
slender stem is from twenty to forty-
five inches tall. The bell-like flowers
are yellow-green and are usually
in pairs. Occasionally, however,
three or four flowers may dangle
together in one cluster.

INDIAN
CUCUMBER-ROOT
Medeola virginiana
Lily Family

This member of the lily family
has two whorls of pointed leaves and
is found in rich damp woods. The
plant varies from one to three feet
in height. The flowers dangle beneath
the top whorl of leaves on large
pedicels. There are six greenish-
yellow petals that curve backwards
and three red-orange stigmas that
curve backwards and are longer than
the petals. Six reddish stamens
protrude from the center. The fruit
is a dark blue or purplish berry
one-fourth to one-half inch in
diameter.

173

CARRION-FLOWER

Smilax herbacea

Lily Family

Carrion-flower is a freely branched shrub which climbs by tendrils. It grows in moist soil of open woods, roadsides, and thickets and is often as long as six feet. The leaves are rounded or heart-shaped at the base but are pointed at the tip. They are very broad and have nerves which run lengthwise and also veins which are not running lengthwise. The leaves are pale green and have a gray-green waxy substance which may be rubbed off. The small yellow-green flowers have six petals and are arranged in umbels which arise from the axils of the leaves. The flowers emit an odor of carrion (rotting flesh). The male (staminate) flowers are on one plant and the female (pistilate) flowers are on another.

GREENBRIER

Smilax rotundifolia

Lily Family

This high-climbing shrub grows in open woods, thickets, and along roadsides. It has a green, four-angl stem which is scattered with stout thorns. The vine is often evergreer and climbs by means of tendrils. The leathery leaves are a shiny greer color and are broadly triangular or heart-shaped.

They have lengthwise nerves plus net-like veins. The part of the stem which bears the flower cluster arises from the axil of the leaves. The staminate flowers and the pistilate flowers are on separate plant The berries are blue-black.

White Mandarin and Liverberry are two other common names given to this plant. It grows in cold, moist woods and thickets to a height of from one to three feet.

A distinctive characteristic to look for when trying to distinguish this Twisted Stalk from other Twisted Stalks, is the sharp kink in the tiny flower stalks.

White Mandarin has a zig-zag stem with alternate, oval, pointed leaves which embrace the stem. A single bell-shaped flower (rarely two) hangs on a kinked stalk below each leaf. Read page 76 under Rose Twisted Stalk to see how flowers are attached. The flowers are generally greenish-white and the petals and sepals are about one-half inch long. The insides of the petals are often spotted with purple. The tips of the petals turn backwards. The fruit is a bright, fleshy, inedible berry.

TWISTED STALK
Streptopus amplexifolius
Lily Family

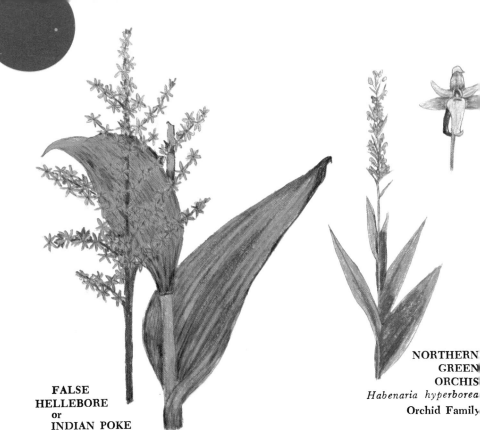

FALSE
HELLEBORE
or
INDIAN POKE
Veratrum viride
Lily Family

This stout plant is from two to
six feet tall and can be found
growing in low wet land or swamps.
It has a single stem with broad,
clasping leaves which are heavily
ribbed in a length-wise direction.
Leaves are alternate on the stem.
The yellow-green flowers have
six petals and are star-shaped.
They are arranged in a large,
much-branched panicle at the
summit of the stem.   Each flower
is about two-thirds of an inch broad.
All parts of this plant are highly
poisonous.

NORTHERN
GREEN
ORCHIS
Habenaria hyperborea
Orchid Family

This tall, leafy orchis grows in bogs,
woods, and thickets to a height
of from eight to forty inches.
The flowers are green or yellowish-gre
and are in a compact spike-like
raceme with small leaf-like bracts
intermingled with the flowers.
The three sepals at the back of
the flower are larger than the two
side petals.   The side petals are long
and narrow and are directed forwar
The lower petal forms a lip.   There
a spur about the same length as the li
which curves inward towards the stem

Hooker's Orchid grows in woods to a height of from eight to sixteen inches. It has two large, roundish leaves which are up to six inches long and five inches wide.
The orchid-like flowers are yellowish-green and have a long tapering spur at the base. The spur may be nearly an inch long. The sepals and lip are about one-half inch long, but the side petals are much shorter. Flowers are arranged in a slender raceme at the top of the stem. There are no bracts on the stem and the flowers are not on separate pedicels (stems), but attached directly to the main stem.

HOOKER'S ORCHID
Habenaria hookeri
Orchid Family

This is a branching weed which should not be touched because it is covered with coarse, stinging hairs. It grows in waste ground where the soil is light or loosely packed.
It has a hollow, four-angled stem which is from two to four feet. The stem is fibrous but gives off a watery juice if it is broken.
The alternate leaves have long stalks and are coarsely toothed.
The tiny greenish flowers have four petal-like parts. They are in branching clusters which originate in the leaf axils. The staminate (male) and the pistillate (female) flowers are often on separate plants.

STINGING NETTLE
Utrica dioica
Nettle Family

SOUR DOCK or CURLED DOCK
Rumex crispus
Buckwheat Family

There are several docks in our area. The one shown is a stout erect plant that grows along roads and in wastelands to a height of from one to four feet. It has many stem which are tough and fibrous and have a corky center. The leaves have a prominent midrib on the under side and the margins are ver wavy. The large pea-green flower cluster at the ends of the branches is made up of many smaller branchi clusters. There are small leaves intermingled with the winged flowe There is a brown fringe around the stem at the axils of the leaves. Each seed has three broad, heart-shaped wings and the three-sided seed is enclosed in this papery structure.

Sheep Sorrel grows in acid soil in wastelands, roadsides, and unkept lawns, to a height of from four to twelve inches. The stem is erect and may be either simple or branched. The leaves are variable, but are usually arrowhead-shaped with three lobes. They have a very acid or sour taste. The flower heads are very minute and are in small clusters separated by empty spaces on the stem. The flowers are green, but often turn reddish-brown as they mature. Male flowers are yellow. Sometimes the spike-like flower cluster is half as tall as the entire plant.

SHEEP SORREL or RED SORREL
Rumex acetosella
Buckwheat Family

GARDEN SORREL or GREEN SORREL
Rumex acetosa
Buckwheat Family

This sorrel is larger than Sheep Sorrel and the upper leaves clasp the stem. The lower lobes of the leaf point backwards. The flower spikes are larger and more compact. This sorrel grows in fields and along roads to a height from six to twenty-four inches.

Lamb's Quarters — also called
Pigweed — is a branching weed
with stout red-streaked stems.
It grows in fields, gardens, and in
wastelands to a height of from
one to three feet. The upper stem
leaves are thin, long, slender, but
untoothed. The basal leaves are
large, diamond-shaped, coarsely
toothed, and mealy-white on the
underside. The small greenish
flowers are in dense clusters on
separate stems which grow from
axils of leaves.

LAMB'S QUARTERS
Chenopodium album
Goosefoot Family

There are several species of orache
in our area. Most are weedy plants
which grow to a height of up to
forty inches. The plant is mealy
and is often reddish. The leaves
have petioles and are either opposite
or alternate on the stem.
The flowers are in the upper nodes
on nearly leafless spikes.
Both staminate and pistillate flowers
are intermingled. Orache grows
in alkaline soil and wastelands.

ORACHE
Atriplex patula
Goosefoot Family

This erect plant is from six to
twenty-four inches tall and is branched
from the base. It grows in woodland
clearings, along roads, and in wastelands.
It is often found in great quantity
after a fire. The basal leaves have
long leaf stems (petioles) which
are often longer than the blade itself,
but the upper stem leaves have very
short petioles. The leaves are
triangular in general outline, but
have irregular teeth. The flowers
are in tight, round clusters at the
top of the stem and in axils of
upper leaves. When in the seed stage,
the fruit looks like a bright, red berry.

STRAWBERRY-BLITE
Chenopodium capitatum
Goosefoot Family

179

DWARF GLASSWORT
Salicornia bigelovii
Goosefoot Family

This glasswort is a flashy pea-green
plant with a few to many spreading
branches. It has sections or joints
which are wider than they are long.
It grows from two to twelve inches
tall in salt marshes.
The minute flowers are in groups
of three and are sunk in grooves
in the fleshy spike above the axils
of the over-lapping scale-like bracts.

KNAWEL
Scleranthus annuus
Pink Family

SLENDER GLASSWORT
Salicornia europaea
Goosefoot Family

This glasswort is the most common
species found in salt marshes or
in salty, inland soil. It may be
either erect or sprawling and is a
more slender plant than the
Dwarf Glasswort is. The joints are
longer than they are wide — just
the opposite of the one above.
The flowers are in groups of three
in the joints, but the central flower
is broader than the two side ones.

WOODY GLASSWORT
Salicornia virginica
Goosefoot Family

This glasswort often forms large
mats in salt marshes. It has creepin
woody stems which take root at the
nodes and send up single, erect
flowering stems from four to twelve
inches tall. The flowering stems
are fleshy and the scale-like bracts
with tiny flowers inside are only
at the tips of the stems.

This tiny, wiry, bushy plant grows
in wastelands to a height of from
one to six inches. It is an annual
weed which dies at the end of each
season. It has a slender stem which
is forked and contains many thin,
opposite leaves. The flower has no
petals, but a five-lobed green calyx
which holds the stamens and pistil.
The mature seed is straw-colored.

EARLY MEADOW RUE
Thalictrum dioicum
Buttercup Family

This plant grows from one to three
feet high in moist, thin woodlands.
It is much shorter than the
Tall Meadow Rue which blooms
later in the season.
Early Meadow Rue has drooping
flowers and drooping foliage.
The staminate flowers (male) are
on one plant and the pistillate (female)
flowers are on another. The male and
female flowers look very different from

PURPLE MEADOW-RUE
Thalictrum dasycarpum
Buttercup Family

Purple Meadow-Rue is a larger and
less fragile looking plant than
Early Meadow-Rue. It, too, has
female and male flowers on different
plants. It is pictured here in the
fruiting stage, but the flowers are
very similar to those of the
Early Meadow-Rue.
This plant grows in wet meadows,
swamps, and along streams to a
height of from three to six feet.
It often has a purple stem with a
whitish powdery substance on the
stem and leaves.
The underside of the leaves are
covered with fine down.

each other. (See the enlargement.)
The color of the male flower is really
the color of its many stamens which
hang down, for the greenish sepals
fall soon after they open and
the plant has no petals.
The female flower is small and has
four light green petal-like sepals
with several small pistils in the center.
These pistils develop into dry, hard,
symmetrical seed pods with a single
seed in each one. The leaves have
long main stalks and the small
leaflets are thin and not veiny or waxy.
The leaflets are in sets of three and
each individual leaflet is three-lobed.

181

CYPRESS SPURGE
Euphorbia cyparissias
Spurge Family

Cypress Spurge grows in dense masses
along roads, in fields, and cemeteries,
and around foundations of old
buildings. The stems are from six
to twelve inches tall and have
a great number of needle-like, pale-
green leaves. The flowers are clustered
together at the summit of each plant.
Each odd-looking flower cluster
(see inset) is above a pair of yellow
petal-like bracts which may turn
red with age.

BLUE COHOSH
or PAPOOSE-ROOT
Caulophyllum thalictroides
Barberry Family

This is a stout plant which grows
in moist, rich woods to a height
of from one to three feet.
The stem bears a single leaf, but it is
so large and is so divided that it has
the appearance of many leaves.
The flowers are greenish yellow
to brownish-yellow and are arranged
in a large terminal cluster.
Each flower has six tiny petals and
six larger sepals — the star-like sepals
are more showy than the smaller petals.
There are six stamens and a single
yellow pistil. The flowers are later
replaced by clusters of deep blue
"berries" which are not berries at all,
but merely seeds with a fleshy
outer layer.

182

LEAFY SPURGE
Euphorbia esula
Spurge Family

Leafy Spurge resembles the spurge above, but is taller and less leafy. The narrow leaves are broader than those of the Cypress Spurge, and there are not as many leaves on the stem. There are numerous smaller alternating bracts *below the top* flower umbel, whereas the flowers of the Cypress Spurge are all at the top. Though the illustration does not indicate, the Leafy Spurge is much larger than the Cypress Spurge.

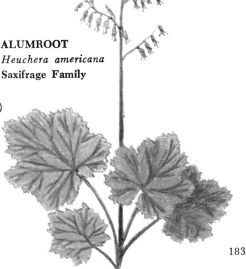

This plant grows in dry or rocky woods and on shaded banks to a height of from two to three feet. The leaves are chiefly basal and have hair on the underside. The leaves are on long stems (petioles) and are from three to four inches wide and have from seven to nine round-toothed lobes. The flowers are greenish-yellow and are in elongated panicles at the top of the leafless stem. Five small green petals alternate with the five lobes of the calyx. There are five stamens with orange tips which are much longer than the rest of the flower.

ALUMROOT
Heuchera americana
Saxifrage Family

183

GREEN VIOLET
Cubelium concolor
Violet Family

Though this coarse, downy plant belongs to the violet family, it is nothing like the violet which comes to most people's mind. The plant is from one to three feet tall and grows in rich woods and lowlands. The leaves are long and pointed, often with a few small teeth on the sides as it narrows to a point. The greenish-white flowers are in pairs or singly in a drooping position from the leaf axils. Each flower has its own hairy stem. The petals and sepals are alike in both size and color, but the lowest petal is sac-like, as the lowest of other violets is. The clublike pistil is also very similar to the pistil of other violets.

ENGLISH PLANTAIN
Plantago lanceolata
Plantain Family

COMMON PLANTAIN
Plantago major
Plantain Family

Common Plantain grows in dooryards, lawns, and in waste places to a height of from six to eighteen inches. It has thick, broad, dull-green leaves at the base of the plant. The leaf stalks are grooved and are often longer than the leaf blade.

The leaf stalks are tough and dull green, but are very green at the base. The tiny flowers are in long, tight-clustered flower spikes.

FEVERWORT
Triosteum perfoliatum
Honeysuckle Family

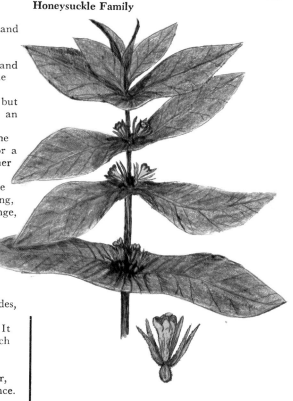

This unattractive plant has many common names, some of which are: Feverwort, Wild Coffee, Horse-Gentian, and Tinker's-Weed. The plant grows in rocky, open woods and clearings to a height of from two to four feet. The paired leaves narrow abruptly at the center and join together around the stem. The stem is downy with gland-tipped hairs. The flowers have no stalks, but are set in the axils of the leaf on an egg-shaped ovary which is below each flower. (See enlargement). The petals are greenish, a dull yellow, or a dull purple, and are joined together to make a funnel-shaped hairy flower with five erect lobes. The flower is surrounded by five, long, hairy sepals. The fruit is a red-orange, hairy, berry-like cluster with three nutlets.

English Plantain is a weed which grows in dooryards, along roadsides, and in wastelands to a height of from nine to twenty-four inches. It has slender three-ribbed leaves which taper at both ends. The grooved stalk has a short, dense spike of flowers at the top. When in flower, the cluster has a bushy appearance.

SEASIDE PLANTAIN
Plantago maritima
Plantain Family

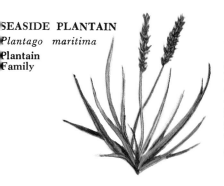

Seaside Plantain grows in tufts on shores, rocky cliffs, and on seaside ledges to a height of from two to eight inches. It has thick, fleshy, linear leaves with a groove in the center. The flower stalk is shorter than that on the English Plantain, but the flower head is longer. The leaves of this plant are often called "Goosetongues" and are picked to be cooked as greens.

185

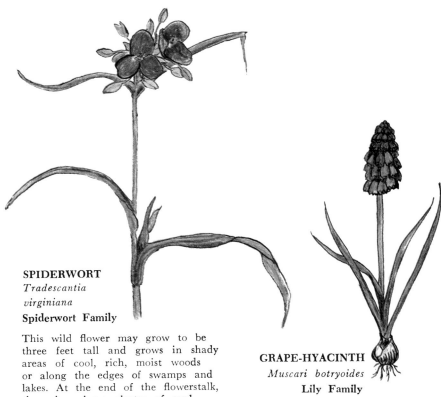

SPIDERWORT
*Tradescantia
virginiana*
Spiderwort Family

This wild flower may grow to be
three feet tall and grows in shady
areas of cool, rich, moist woods
or along the edges of swamps and
lakes. At the end of the flowerstalk,
there is a large cluster of oval
greenish buds which open one or two
at a time. As one flower fades,
other buds will open. The flowers
are usually blue, but may be
violet, rose, and rarely white. Each
flower has three large petals and
six showy yellow stamens which
protrude from the center. The flower
itself is between one and two inches
wide. The leaves are long and
pointed. They are shiny green in
color and grow to be a foot or more
in length.

GRAPE-HYACINTH
Muscari botryoides
Lily Family

Two species of this plant grow in
our area, but both are very similar.
From a bulb in the ground, a single
slender stem grows and bears a
dense tapering cluster of small barrel-
like blue flowers. Sometimes the
very tips of the bells have a white
margin — sometimes they are plain.
The slender, flat, grass-like leaves
have a pale groove in the center. The
entire plant is usually less than ten
inches tall.

he Twisted Stalk has sharply-pointed
aves arranged alternately along a
zag forked stem. The flowers
e bell-shaped and about one-half
ch long. They have six pointed
nk or purplish petals which curve
wards only at the tips.

he flowers do not hang from the
ils of the leaf as in most plants,
t grow from the side of the stem
posite the leaf. The flower stalk
en doubles back so that the flower
ngs beneath the leaf.

other Twisted Stalk is on page 175
the white section.

PINK MANDARIN or ROSE TWISTED STALK
Streptopus roseus
Lily Family

PICKEREL WEED
Pontederia cordata
Pickerel Weed Family

Pickerel Weed is an aquatic herb
which is frequently found along
borders of ponds, streams, and shallow
lakes. It appears to grow on top of
the water, but actually is embedded
in the mud beneath the water. The
thick flowering stems are erect
and from one to four feet tall. The
leaves are arrowhead-shaped and
from two to ten inches long and
from one to six inches wide. The
leaves are thick, glossy, and dark
green.

The numerous flowers are violet-blue
and are arranged in a dense spike.
Each flower is tubular and about
one-fourth of an inch long. It is
curbed and has two lips. The
upper lip has three lobes, the middle
of which is the largest. There
are two yellow spots at the base of
this lobe within the flower. The lower
lip has three linear spreading lobes.

SLENDER
BLUE-EYED GRASS
Sisyrinchium mucronatum
Iris Family

There are so many species of this wild flower that a beginner would do better to learn to recognize only the genus, and not try to identify all of the different species of Blue-Eyed Grass. Blue-Eyed Grass is a stiff, grass-like plant that thrives in moist meadows and pastures. It grows to be ten or twelve inches high. The delicate star-like flowers vary in color from white through blue to pale violet, but they all have yellow centers which look like eyes. The flowers are about one-half inch across and are located at the end of a long stem which is usually taller than the leaves.

The light green leaves are narrow and grass-like and are very close to the stems. The stems and leaves differ from ordinary grasses in that they are quite stiff and flattened. Several buds seem to pop out of a leaf bract at the top of the leaf-like stem. These tiny round buds do not open at the same time.

BLUE FLAG
Iris versicolor
Iris Family

Blue Flag is a showy plant which grows in marshes, stream borders, and other wet places. The stems are round, smooth, erect, and from two to three feet tall. The leaves are usually shorter than the flower and are mainly on the lower part of the stem or at the base of the plant. The flowers are violet blue and have six clawed segments which are joined together at the center to make a tube. The three outer parts are variegated with yellow and white and are beautifully veined with purple. They curve down and inwards. The upper three are smaller and curve upwards and inwards over the center of the plant.

PURPLE VIRGIN'S BOWER
Clematis verticillaris
Buttercup Family

This trailing, climbing vine is a rare perennial which grows in rocky woods and thickets. What at first appear to be four almost transparent blue-veined petals are really sepals. They are downy on the inside and the outside. They never really open, but remain in a cup-shaped position. The flower would measure from two to four inches if opened fully. When the blossom fades, the styles become elongated and feathery and give the vine the appearance of a nest. The leaves have three parts. Each part has unequal teeth on the margin and a sharp point at the tip.

HEPATICA
Hepatica americana
Buttercup Family

Hepaticas are one of our earliest spring flowers and often spring forth from among the fallen leaves on the woodland floor before the last of the winter snows have melted. They seem to be well prepared for the cool spring days, for they are clustered together and have fuzzy hairs on their stems and buds. The new flowers open while last year's leaves are still covering the root of the plant. New leaves appear after the flowers fade. Leaves are deeply three-lobed, are green at first, but turn leathery and mottled green-purple later in the fall. The shape and color of the old leaves near the ground remind some of a liver, and has given rise to the name of Liverwort.

No two clusters of hepaticas are exactly alike. Some are scented while others are not. The colors vary from pink, to blue, to lavender, and even to white. The showy part of the flower is not petals, but colored sepals. There are from six to eight sepals and many pistils and stamens in the center. These turn green after fertilization and give a porcupine appearance to the end of the stem.

PURPLE AVENS
Geum rivale
Rose Family

The Purple Avens grows to be from
one to three feet tall. It may be
found growing in bogs, swamps, or
wet meadows all across the Northern
United States and Canada.
The slender brown stem has a cluster
of nodding purple-white flowers at
the end. They are somewhat cup-
shaped. Each blossom is about an
inch broad. The brown sepals are
clearly visible on the outside of the
flower. The flowers hang down
from the tips of the stem.
The leaves are quite different from
those of other plants. The larger
leaves at the bottom of the plant   are
jagged and tooth-edged. Each
leaf has five main parts. The bottom
two parts are paired, the middle two
parts are paired, but the fifth part
is at the tip of the stem and is much
larger than the other four parts. Four
tiny insignificant leaves are paired
on the stem between the larger
pairs of leaf parts.

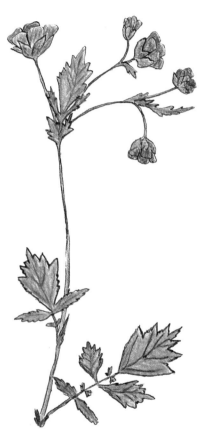

WILD LUPINE
Lupinus perennis
Pea Family

This plant grows straight upwards in dry or moist sandy soil in open areas and along road sides. It is often as tall as two feet. The leaves are arranged in groups of from seven to ten segments which extend outwards from a central point. The numerous blue flowers are arranged in racemes at the top of the plant. The flowers are pea-like with the bottom lip about twice as long as the top one.

ALFALFA
Medicago sativa
Pea Family

This plant is low and is often found lying along the ground. It is as long as one and one-half feet and grows in fields and along roadsides. It is often grown as a forage crop for cattle. The leaves are clover-like and in groups of three. The tube-shaped flowers are from one-fourth to one-half inch long and vary from blue to violet. Each flower is on its own tiny stem called a pedicel, but gathered together into a cluster. One distinguishing feature is the seed pod which twists or coils into a spiral. It has from one to three complete turns and is covered with fine hair.

BLUE VETCH
Vicia cracca
Pea Family

The stems of this plant are climbing or trailing and are up to a yard long. Blue Vetch grows in fields or meadows and along roadsides. The leaflets are arranged in pairs along a center leaf stalk. There are from five to ten pairs of leaflets on each leaf. Tendrils are at the end of each leaf stalk. The blue flowers are crowded together on flower stems which grow from the leaf axils. Each flower has long triangular-shaped lobes and is less than one-half inch long.

191

EARLY BLUE or WOOD VIOLET

Viola palmata

This violet is covered with long soft hairs. It grows in rich soil in woodlan or on limestone ledges. The leaves ar deeply divided into five to eleven parts. Each part is deeply toothed an the center one is usually widest. Sometimes the early spring leaves a not divided. The flowers are three-fourths to one and one-half inches broad and are usually deep violet wi streaks of white. The two side petals are bearded.

BLUE VIOLETS
Violet Family

There are so many kinds of blue and purple violets that it is difficult for an amateur to tell them apart. These five are similar, but the distinguishing characteristics are given to help in identification.

MARSH BLUE VIOLET
Viola cucullata

The violet in the center of the page is from five to ten inches tall. The flower stems are usually taller than the leaves. It is a smooth plant which is found in wet meadows or near streams, bogs, or springs. The violet-blue petals get darker toward the throat. The lower middle petal is veined and shorter than the other two petals. The two side petals are densely bearded, but the lower middle is smooth.

NEW ENGLAND BLUE VIOLET
Viola novae-angliae

The three lower petals of this violet are all bearded and the color is a more reddish-violet. The leaves are more triangular in shape. It grows in wet places.

COMMON BLUE or MEADOW VIOLET
Viola papilionacea

This violet is from three to eight inches high and is not hairy. It grows in moist fields and damp woods. The very large leaves are dark green, heart-shaped and have toothed margins. The deep blue flowers have five petals. The two side petals are bearded but the bottom middle one is not. The bottom middle petal is narrow and boat shaped.

BIRD-FOOT VIOLET
Viola pedata

This plant is found in dry fields or open woods. The leaf blades are deeply parted with each part having two to four teeth at the tip. The petals are all beardless and the lowest petal is wider and deeply veined. The tips of the large orange stamens are conspicuous at the center. Some varieties of this flower are bi-colored with the two top petals a darker color than the lower three.

LAPLAND RHODODENDRON
Rhododendron lapponicum
Heath Family

This is a dwarf rhododendron which grows in higher elevations of New England and New York. It is a freely branching shrub, not much taller than a foot. The leaves are less than an inch long. The leaves are oval, leathery, evergreen, and are scaly on the underside. The bright purple flowers are in small clusters at the ends of the branches — usually only two or three in a cluster. Each flower is less than three-fourths of an inch broad. The pistils and stamens are very noticeable.

VIOLET WOOD-SORREL
Oxalis violacea
Wood-Sorrel Family

This small delicate plant is found in open woods and rocky banks. It seldom grows taller than eight inches. The leaves are heart-shaped and are arranged in groups of threes. The leaflets often fold along a center crease and hang down in a closed position. Sometimes the leaves are reddish on the underside. From three to twelve rose-purple flowers are on each plant. Each flower is about three-fourths of an inch long and is veined with pink or purple.

PERIWINKLE or MYRTLE
Vinca minor
Dogbane Family

This tiny trailing plant has escaped from gardens and cemeteries and is now found in woods in masses as a "wild flower." It has shiny evergreen leaves which are opposite on the stem. The plant is a creeping, spreading ground cover, and is rarely taller than six or eight inches. The purplish-blue flowers are about an inch broad. The five petals are arranged in a perfectly symmetric pattern with the white centers meeting to form a perfect star in the middle and a tubular throat.

BLUETS or QUAKER LADIES
Houstonia caerulea
Bedstraw Family

This dainty light blue or purple flower is found all over fields in New England in the spring. Sometimes they grow so thick, that when

viewed from a distance, they give the appearance of snow. The plant is usually about three inches high and grows right in together with grass, violets, and other field wild flowers. The tiny stems are slender, and pointed leaves are arranged in pairs along the stems. The basal leaves are larger and are clustered about at the base of the plant, but often hidden in the grass. The flowers have four petals which vary from white, to blue, to lavender. The petals are joined to form a tube which opens to make a face about three-eighths of an inch wide. The flower has a bright yellow eye, and appears at the end of the stem.

Blue Phlox is an erect plant from ten to twenty inches high which grows in fields and in rich, moist woods. It has long opposite leaves along the sticky, hairy stem. The flowers vary in color from pale blue to red-purple and sometimes white. The fragrant flowers have five wedge-shaped petals which are sometimes notched at the tips. The flowers are loosely arranged at the top of the stem and radiate outward from the center.

BLUE PHLOX
Phlox divaricata
Phlox Family

Jacob's Ladder is found in wooded swamps, bogs, and along streams. The stout erect stem is hairy and from one to three feet tall. The loose clusters of blue-violet bells are at the ends of the branches. The five white-tipped stamens protrude noticeably from the center of the blossom. Each flower has five rounded blue lobes and a white center with wine-colored veins in it. The leaves are subdivided into untoothed leaflets. There are from four to nine pairs of sharply pointed leaflets and an odd leaflet at the tip of the leaf stalk.

JACOB'S LADDER
Polemonium vanbruntiae
Phlox Family

MOSS PHLOX
or MOSS-PINK
Phlox subulata
Phlox Family

This plant varies greatly in color from white to pink to blue-purple. See page 115 in the pink section for a description.

BLUEBELLS
*Mertensia
virginica*
**Forget-Me-Not
Family**

Other names for this plant are Mertensia, Virginia Cowslip, and Virginia Bluebells. It grows from eight inches to two feet in moist lowlands and woods near rivers. The nodding funnel-like flowers are pink while in bud, but are blue when fully opened. The tube is longer than the flower face. The leaves are oval, smooth, and strongly veined. The flowers are from three-fourths to one inch long. The stem is smooth and juicy.

TRUE FORGET-ME-NOT
Myosotis scorpioides

This small plant has delicate flowers with five sky-blue petals and a yellow eye. The flower is less than one-third of an inch across. The stem forks at the top and has two coiled clusters of buds. As the buds open, the cluster uncoils. The hairy, blunt leaves are attached directly to the hairy stem on alternate sides. Forget-Me-Not grows along brooks and in cool wet places to a height of from six to twenty-four inches, but an average plant is usually less than a foot high.

This plant is a close relative of Bluebells in the top left of the page, but instead of standing erect, it lies on the ground and often forms thick mats. The spoon-shaped leaves are thick, fleshy, and hairless. They are said to have a taste similar to the taste of oysters. The flowers are pink at first, but later turn blue. They are about one-third of an inch long, and the tube is longer than the face of the flower. This plant grows on beaches and rocks along the coast and has stems up to forty inches long.

COMFREY
*Symphytum
officinale*
**Forget-Me-Not
Family**

See page 116 in the pink secti for details.

**SEA MERTENSIA
or OYSTERLEAF**
Mertensia maritima
**Forget-Me-Not
Family**

GROUND IVY or
GILL-OVER-THE-GROUND
Glechoma hederacea
Mint Family

The Ground Ivy is a lovely little trailing mint that can be found growing in damp places, fields, and unmowed lawns around old buildings and trees or stumps. It usually appears in patches and blooms along with purple violets, which grow in the same places.

The trumpet-shaped blossoms are blue or light purple and are located in the axils of the leaves. The blossoms are about 1/2 inch long. The upper lip stands erect and is notched in the center. The lower lip has three spreading lobes which are spotted with dark purple.

The leaves have a heart-shaped base and are deeply scalloped or toothed along the edges. The leaves are arranged in pairs along the stem. Their surface is downy and the veins are very noticeable. The leaves vary in size, depending upon the richness of the soil and how early in the spring they appear. Those which appear later in the spring often have leaves which are more than an inch broad, while those blooming very early have tiny leaves.

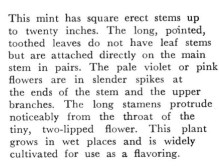

SPEARMINT
Mentha spicata
Mint Family

This mint has square erect stems up to twenty inches. The long, pointed, toothed leaves do not have leaf stems but are attached directly on the main stem in pairs. The pale violet or pink flowers are in slender spikes at the ends of the stem and the upper branches. The long stamens protrude noticeably from the throat of the tiny, two-lipped flower. This plant grows in wet places and is widely cultivated for use as a flavoring.

BLUE GIANT
HYSSOP
Agastache foeniculum
Mint Family

This plant has erect, branching stems up to forty inches tall. It grows in dry upland woods. Blue tubular flowers are in spikes at the top of the stem and at the ends of the branches. They also appear as little pin-cushion-like clusters in axils of upper leaves. The tiny flower has two pairs of protruding stamens. Two stamens point upwards and two stamens point downwards. The pistil extends straight outward. (See enlargement). The leaves are toothed and pointed at the tip, but are very broad or rounded at the base. The leaves emit an odor of anise and are wooly white on the underside.

This is a common creeping weed which is from four to twenty-four inches tall and grows in just about any type of soil. The hairy leaves are in pairs, but vary greatly in shape. Usually they are long with a blunt point at the tip. The tubular, two-lipped flowers are arranged in cylindrical spikes at the top of the plant. The flowers protrude from among many wide bracts. The color of the flowers varies from violet-blue to pink or even white and the color of the bracts varies from shades of brown to shades of red or green.

SELF HEAL
or HEAL-ALL
Prunella vulgaris
Mint Family

DOWNY WOOD MINT
Blephilia ciliata
Mint Family

This mint grows in moist and dry woods to a height of from one to three feet. The leaves are almost stalkless and have white down on the bottom. The flowers are pale blue with purple spots. They are in whorls in a cylindrical head, but are separated by a row of fringed, dark-colored bracts. The two-lipped flower has an untoothed, hood-like upper lip and a three-lobed bottom lip.

CATNIP
Nepeta cataria
Mint Family

Catnip has paired leaves, square stems, and tubular two-lipped flowers which are characteristic of members of the mint family. It is a hairy, much-branched plant which grows in waste places to a height of six to thirty-six inches. The leaves are arrow-shaped and are on long stems which are about half as long as the leaf itself. The edges are very jagged. The flower cluster may be in a continuous cylindrical shape, or may be interrupted by bare places on the stalks. The flowers are dull white or pale violet and the lower lobes are dotted with purple.

LYRE-LEAVED SAGE
Salvia lyrata
Mint Family

This mint is from one to two feet tall and grows in upland woods and thickets. Most of the leaves are in a ring around the base of the stem and are very irregularly cleft. There is usually only one pair of leaves on the stem. The flowers are either blue or violet and are about an inch long. They are arranged in whorls around the stem. The whorls of flowers are separated by bare places on the stem. The flower is two lipped and the bottom lip is larger than the upper one. The calyx is very hairy and ribbed.

**MARSH
SKULLCAP**
*Scutellaria
epilobiifolia*
Mint Family

This species grows in swampy
thickets, at shores, or in wet meadows
to a height of from one to three
feet. It has single pale-violet or blue
flowers which grow in the leaf axils.
The leaves are very short-stalked
or even stalkless — attached directly
to the main stem. The leaves are
slightly toothed, and more yellow-
green in color than the other species.

SHOWY SKULLCAP
Scutellaria serrata
Mint Family

Showy Skullcap grows in woods and
on banks and is from eight to
twenty-four inches tall. The leaves
are large, ovate, and toothed. They
get smaller as the plant tapers
to the top. The smooth blue flowers
are arranged in a terminal raceme.
Each flower is about an inch long,
has two lips, and a small protuberance
on the upperside of the calyx.
This is shaped like a skullcap —
hence the name.

SMALLER SKULLCAP
Scutellaria parvula
Mint Family

This small skullcap is from three
to twelve inches in height and grows
in sandy or limy soil or in upland
woods. The hairy leaves have two or
three scallops on each side. Most of
the veins on the leaves run
lengthwise. The stems are very hairy
and branching. Small bluish-purple
flowers about one-third inch long are
arranged singly at leaf axils.

HORSE-NETTLE
Solanum carolinense
Nightshade Family

Horse-Nettle is a large branching plant which grows in sandy soils, fields, and in waste places. It grows to a height of from one to four feet. The stems are erect and very spiny.
The leaves are rough and have from two to five large teeth on each side. The central rib or vein of the leaf is also spiny.
There are several flowers together in one cluster. Each flower has five pale violet or white petals which are curved backwards from the yellow-orange cluster of anthers in the center.

Bittersweet — also called Purple Nightshade — is a weak climbing or reclining vine-like plant which grows in moist thickets throughout our area. The stem is often as long as six or eight feet. The flowers are similar to Horse-Nettle, but are smaller. The five swept-back violet petals surround the orange beak-like center. The top leaves are simple and pointed, but the larger lower leaves have two small lobes at the base. The fruit is a red, egg-shaped berry which is borne in drooping clusters.

BITTERSWEET
Solanum dulcamara
Nightshade Family

COMMON SPEEDWELL
Veronica officinalis
Snapdragon Family

This speedwell is found in dry fields and in upland woods. It is hairy and the stems are reclining or creeping. It is less than ten inches high. The hairy leaves are toothed and have a narrow base. They are oblong and about two inches long. The flowers are blue and are about one-fourth inch across. Three of the petals are round, but the lower petal is smaller and narrower. There are two stamens protruding noticeably from the center.

THYME-LEAVED SPEEDWELL
Veronica serpyllifol
Snapdragon Family

This speedwell is similar to the one at left, but does not have any hair. The leaves are very small — seldom over one-half of an inch long. The are usually not toothed. The flowers are about one-third inch across and sometimes have darker stripes c them. The plant grows in fields, meadows, and on lawns.

AMERICAN BROOKLIME
Veronica americana
Snapdragon Family

This is very similar to the above, but has large toothed, triangular-shaped leaves which are juicy and smooth. It grows near brooks or in swamps and is often as large as twenty inches.

BIRD'S-EYE SPEEDWELL
Veronica chamaedrys
Snapdragon Family

This is similar to the Common Speedwell, but has rounder-shaped leaves which are attached directly the main stem. The leaves are downy and toothed. Bird's-Eye Speedwell grows along roadsides or in moist fields and gardens.

ONE-FLOWERED CANCER-ROOT
Orbanche uniflora
Broomrape Family

This flower may have either light
purple or white flowers. See page
55 in the white section for
details.

BUTTERWORT
Pinguicula vulgaris
Bladderwort Family

A Butterwort is a small plant from
two to six inches tall which grows
on wet rocks and in wet meadows
or bogs. It has a circle of yellowish-
green leaves which are shaped like a
football. The edges of the leaves
usually roll inward. Small insects are
often caught on the greasy surface
of the curled leaves. The solitary
flower at the top of the leafless stem
is very similar to a violet. It has
five purple petals and a spur. It is
about one-half of an inch long.

PURPLE BLADDERWORT
Utricularia purpurea
Bladderwort Family

The Purple Bladderwort grows in
quiet ponds and muddy streams. It
has small pea-like lavender or purple
flowers on a leafless stalk. It grows
to a height of from two to six
inches.
The leaves are like tiny filaments
and are usually submerged in mud or
water. There are tiny bladders
attached to the filaments.
There are from one to four flowers
on the plant. Each is two-lipped.
The upper lip is flat or concave and
the lower lip has three lobes and a
yellow spot at its base.

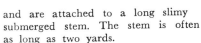

WATERSHIELD
Brasenia schreberi
Water-lily Family

The Watershield grows in ponds and in slow-moving streams. It has oval floating leaves which are from two to four inches long. The leaves are slimy-coated on the bottom and are attached to a long slimy submerged stem. The stem is often as long as two yards.

The plant has small dull purple flowers with either three or four petals and three sepals. Each flower has its own stout flower stalk which is attached to the main stalk.

This wildflower grows as a weed in moist soil, in gardens, and in fields. It stands erect from four to twelve inches high. The basal leaves are about two inches long and are untoothed and spoonshaped. The leaves along the stem are smaller and toothed. The stem leaves have no leaf stems, but are attached directly to the main stem.

The bluish-white flowers are arranged in small flat heads at the tips of the forked stems. There are many small green leaves under each flower head. Each individual flower is minute. The corolla has five nearly equal lobes and is funnel-shaped. The stamens and style protrude from the center of the flower.

This plant is used in salads and as an herb in cooking.

CORNSALAD
Valerianella olitoria
Valerian Family

This plant is from six to eighteen inches high and grows in dry meadows, on cliffs, on beaches, in grassy places. It has wiry hair-like stems and long linear stem leaves. Sometimes the stem is hairy at base. The basal leaves are very small and round, and often wither away before flowering time. There are from one to several nodding bell-shaped flowers at the top. They vary in color from violet blue, to blue, to white.

204

VENUS' LOOKING-GLASS
Specularia perfoliata
Bluebell Family

This erect plant has simple stems from six to thirty inches in height. The leaves are numerous and clasp the stem. The egg-shaped leaves are hairy and are toothed at the edges. The flowers are violet-blue with five spreading lobes. They are from one-half to three-fourths inch broad and are not bell-shaped like the harebell. Each blue flower is tucked individually inside of the cup-like leaf; but occasionally two or three flowers are together. Look for Venus' Looking-Glass in open woods, old fields, and along roadsides.

ROBIN'S-PLANTAIN
Erigeron pulchellus
Composite Family

Robin's Plantain has a hairy stem which forms runners by which the plant spreads to make large colonies. The stem leaves are pointed and either toothed or entire. The basal leaves are widest near the tip, are hairy, and are bluntly toothed. At the top of the stem is a single flower-head or a small cluster of heads — each on its own tiny flower stem. The rays are pale lilac or magenta and the yellow disk in the center is very large.

HAREBELL
Campanula rotundifolia
Bluebell Family

FLAX
Linum
usitatissimum
Flax Family

This delicate slender plant grows in fields and waste places to a height of from nine to thirty inches. The alternate leaves are very narrow and pointed, and have three veins which go lengthwise on the leaf. The flowers have five sepals, five petals, and five stamens. The petals may be blue, white, or yellow, but are most commonly pale blue with a yellow center.

CHICORY
Cichorium
intybus
Composite Family

Chicory grows in fields and along roadsides to a height of four to five feet. It has small, oblong, toothed leaves without stalks along the rigid stem. The basal leaves are similar to the leaves of a dandelion. The blue flower-heads are scattered along the stem and have very little, if any, flower stalk. The blue rays are square-tipped and fringed. Sometimes the flowerhead is pink or white — but most often is clear blue.

BASIL
Satureja vulgaris
Mint Family

Basil has square, creeping stems from which hairy, flowering branches rise from one to two feet. The paired leaves are hairy and slightly toothed. The numerous, tubular, lipped flowe*s* are pale purple or pink. They are in dense heads at the tips of the branche*s* with a pair of leaves below each head. The cluster looks wooly, for there are white hairs on the calyx and bracts.

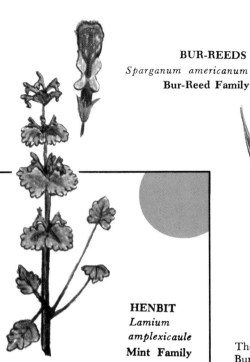

BUR-REEDS
Sparganum americanum
Bur-Reed Family

HENBIT
*Lamium
amplexicaule*
Mint Family

Henbit has several branching square
stems which spring from one root.
It is from four to sixteen inches tall
and grows in wastelands and
along roadsides.
There are a few long-stemmed basil
leaves with scalloped edges.
The wide, stem leaves are roundish
with scalloped edges, and
surround the stem in pairs.
The flowers are clustered in the
axils of the upper leaves.
The tubed flower (see enlargement)
is opened wide at the top and the
upper lip forms a hood over
the lower, lobed lip.
The flower varies from white to
pinkish purple and has darker spots
on it. The upper lip is crowned
with a tuft of magenta hairs.

There are about ten species of
Bur-Reeds in our area and all are
very similar. It would be easiest for
the novice flower collector to call
them all Bur-Reeds, and leave the
determination of species to those who
study botany. Bur-Reeds grow from
one to six feet in marshes, shallow
water, and along borders of ponds
or streams. They are usually erect
plants, but sometimes are floating on
the water. They have grass-like
leaves and pistillate (female) flowers
which form bur-like balls when
they have gone to seed. The staminate
flowers (male) form separate and
smaller balls above the pistillate.

207

COMMON CATTAIL
Typha latifolia
Cattail Family

Cattails grow in ditches along the roads, wet meadows and swamps to a height of from three to six feet. There are many long, flat, narrow leaves at the base. A novice may not consider this a "flower" but the slender brown "cat's-tail" is actually made up of thousands of minute female flowers which are hardly more than a single pistil for each minute flower. Above the cluster of female flowers is a slender spike which is smaller, lighter in color, and which contains the staminate (male) flowers. When the pollen has been dropped to fertilize the female flowers the top flowers die away — leaving only a grayish dry-looking stem.

NARROW-LEAVED CATTAIL
Typha angustifolia
Cattail Family

This cattail is similar to the one above, but can be distinguished by the separation on the stem between the male and female flower clusters. The leaves are narrower and a more yellow-green in color than those on the above cattail.

SKUNK CABBAGE
Symplocarpus foetidus
Arum Family

The Skunk Cabbage is probably New England's earliest spring flower and can be found blooming in bogs and wet places as early as February. It does not look like a flower unless inspected carefully. The hood varies in color from brownish-purple to greenish-yellow, but is usually a mixture of color which gives it a spotted effect. This hood, called a spathe, hides the actual flowers which are in an egg-shaped cluster inside of the hood. The cluster of brownish-yellow flowers is called the spadix and is usually about six inches long. The leaves, which do not appear until the flower has gone to seed, are the more showy part of the plant. They grow to be from one to two feet long and are similar to large cabbage leaves, but are more yellow-green in color.

The "skunk" part of the name comes from the disagreeable odor which is given off by this plant when it is broken or crushed.

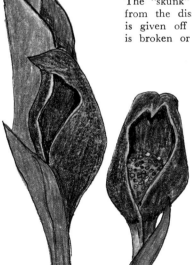

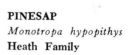

PINESAP
Monotropa hypopithys
Heath Family

See page 156 in the yellow section.

SQUAW-ROOT
Conopholis americana
Broomrape Family

See page 156 in the yellow section.

VIRGINIA SNAKEROOT
Aristolochia serpentaria
Birthwort Family

Virginia Snakeroot grows in woods to a height of from eight to twenty-four inches. An underground stem sends up stalks which bear large heart-shaped leaves and curious-looking flowers. The flowers are solitary on slender, scaly branches at the base of the leafy stem. The flowers may be either dull green or brownish purple, but are usually madder-purple. The flower is s-shaped. It has an enlarged base and flares out at the face to make an irregular three-lobed face. Inside of the throat are six stamens and a pistil. The face is smooth, but the s-shaped throat is hairy.

WILD GINGER
Asarum canadense
Birthwort Family

Wild Ginger has two beautifully
veined leaves and a single red-brown
flower at the base of the stout,
hairy leaf stems. See page 91 in
the red section for further description.

FIGWORT
Scrophularia lanceolata
Snapdragon Family

This erect plant grows in thickets
and at the edge of woods to a
height of from three to eight feet.
The leaves have petioles which seem
to flow into the main stem. The leaf
blades have a pointed tip, a broadly-
rounded base, and sharply toothed
margins. The curious flowers are
arranged in a branching inflorescence
at the summit of the plant. The calyx
is cup-shaped and divided into five
broad lobes. The corolla has two
lips on a wide tube-like throat. The
upper lip has two lobes which lean
forward. The bottom lip has three
lobes, but only the middle one
hangs down. The corolla is a dull
reddish-brown except for the lower
lobe which is a shiny green color.
Note the enlargement of the front and
side view of a single flower.

INDEX TO COMMON NAMES

INDEX TO COMMON NAMES

INDEX TO COMMON NAMES

INDEX TO COMMON NAMES

INDEX TO COMMON NAMES

INDEX TO COMMON NAMES

INDEX TO COMMON NAMES

INDEX OF LATIN NAMES

INDEX OF LATIN NAMES

INDEX OF LATIN NAMES

INDEX OF LATIN NAMES

INDEX OF LATIN NAMES

PINEAPPLE WEED,

see

page 166

224